Leading with Uncommon Courage

JESUS, COFFEE, & PRAYER
Christian Publishing House

Anthology Compiled by Visionary Author:
Tiffany D. Bell

Table of Content

Dedication

To my dearest Ken.
Thank you for teaching me how to love.
Your Love,

A Note from the Publisher of Purpose

Tiffany is an absolute jewel; a woman who has experienced many trials; yet like Maya Angelou's iconic poem~ Still 'She' Rises!

In this authentic compilation of Women from Mississippi to Alaska, and the shores of South Africa too; you will find yourself immersed in the lives of Amazing Women of Faith and Great Wisdom.

If you find yourself needing more courage and strength in this next season; simply seek God first; then open this book... Leading with Uncommon Courage!
These Women have enough courage to fuel a Nation and YOU too.

Cheers to Your Courageous Journey
Min. Nakita Davis
CEO & Founder @jesuscoffeeandprayer

Foreword

Connie Rockco

Picture in your mind's eye a small child adopted by members of the family. Imagine your grandfather and your aunt of the same family passing away and being tossed from pillow to post and trying to gage the temperature of every new family.

As the story about Tiffany Denise Bell unfolds, discover an astonishing decision by one remarkable woman (her mother) made out of love. How one child conceived in darkness and violence, yet carried in love, resulted in a beautiful human being that continues giving love, joy, and understanding. The results of one woman's decision keeps giving life to those that have no voice, like the ocean waters give life.

Experience the pages of the book through Tiffany's eyes as she expresses how God never leaves us through our many trials and tribulations. Feel her pain and relish in the warmth of peace and harmony that God gave to Tiffany as she grew in strength.

As the child of God, who was waiting on permission to be who He intended her to be, this story tells how God prepares to give Tiffany Bell permission to be who she is and know her mission in life.

Journey to
UnCommon Courage

~ Tiffany D Bell

It was an early Thursday morning. My husband was sitting on the side of the bed, telling me softly that it was time to wake up. He was already dressed. I had gotten to bed a little later than usual the night before and really wanted to continue to sleep.

"Tiff," he said, "You've got to get going. You are going to be late to work." I slowly came to my senses. I looked up at him as he smiled and bent over to kiss my forehead.

I met Ken after his car flipped while on a road trip to his hometown near Myrtle Beach, South Carolina. His family had agreed to meet there for Thanksgiving. It was almost love at first sight. We hit it off instantly. Within two weeks, he told me that he knew that he was going to marry me. Five months later, we tied the knot! I packed my things and moved to Mississippi. He was the love of my life.

Even after I had fully awakened, I was incredibly stressed this morning. I felt terribly uneasy. I did not really know why, though. I also did not have time to think much about it. I hurriedly dressed for work. I did not allow myself to acknowledge it. Our regular routine was that Ken would take the kids to school on his way to his job. After getting dressed, I gathered my things and headed out the door. I hesitated for a moment. I thought, "Should I kiss Ken good-bye or just get on the road?" I cannot remember what I decided.

Once I arrived at work, I felt as if I should give Ken a call. "Why?" I wondered. It just did not make sense. I called him a few times. No answer. About 10:00 A.M. I sent him a text that said, "I love you." Still, the feeling would not go away. By 2:00 P.M. that day, I could not take it anymore. I had a powerful urge to be near Ken. It was all that I could think about.

My boss let me leave early. It was nearly 2:30.

I did not know where to head. I just knew that I needed to find him. I drove over a block near the mall and picked up my phone to give him a call again. This time, a woman answered. That had never happened before. I identified myself to her and asked for Ken. She did not answer me. I could hear her say, "Doctor, this is his wife."

Shortly after, the doctor began to speak.

"Ma'am, I am an ER doctor with Biloxi Regional Medical Center. Your husband has had an accident." I immediately asked if he was alright. After three times of asking him, he finally said that my family and I should come to the hospital to say our good-byes.

Never in a million years did I see that coming. Ken was only 34 years old. He was young, vibrant, wise, loving, and kind. He was the kind of guy that people were drawn to. He accepted everyone. Ken believed strongly in community and taking care of the needs of family, friends, and strangers alike. He loved being a father. Ken knew that since age five, that he wanted to be a dad. He also had an excellent relationship with his mom. He cherished her and wanted to take care of her as she entered retirement age. We thought that we would grow old together. We were supposed to be that nearly ninety-year-old couple holding hands on an evening stroll.

When I ended the call with the doctor, I yelled at God. I said, "This is not what you promised. This is not a part of the plan!" My entire future was lost. How was I going to take care of two boys? I lived 700 miles away from my family. His family lived even farther away. What was I going to do?

I grew quiet. I sat for several minutes, trying to formulate a plan. I had to tell my kids. How was I going to tell his mom? The doctor wanted me to come and identify his body. I knew that that was not going to happen. If I did not know anything else, I knew that I would preserve my last memories of him. I was going to remember how helpful he was as we worked to get the boys ready for school that morning. I would remember hearing him singing in the shower. What was I supposed to do about his business? His equipment? The rental houses? All of that would need to be taken care of. It was all so much to deal with.

At this point, I began to address the Lord again. I also knew that my attitude needed an adjustment. I remember telling Him that if this were how things would be, He was responsible for making sure that everything the boys and I needed would be taken care of. It was too much for me to handle. I honestly felt that He was obligated to take care of us.

And, of course, He did.

Immediately, people poured in from all around to help us. Ken was well known among his military family and church family. So many blessings came our way, I could hardly keep up. Not a single thing went undone that year. The comfort and love that we were shown made a difference in my heart.

I learned a lot about myself in Ken's death. I realized that I had lived a self-focused life. I loved God, but I cannot say that I really loved my neighbor. Ken tried teaching me small lessons over the years about love... how to communicate it, how to receive it, and how to reciprocate it. It was not until he died that the lessons began to sink in. I began to want to do more with my life and to do more for my community. But I was afraid. I really did not know where to start or really what it meant to be more, do more, or give more. I had spent so many years living to survive. I did not know what it really meant to thrive.

If you consider having a lot of possessions thriving, then yes, we were thriving. We owned several vehicles, houses, a business. But I did not know the real *Tiffany*. Who was I outside of the kids and Ken? I was a timid girl that was filled with fear and plagued by insecurity. What was I supposed to do to move forward? Could I do something more with my life? And if so, how? Where would I start? Slowly I began to take baby steps toward developing a life that did not revolve solely around me.

That is how this book came to be.

I decided that I would intentionally comfort people with the same comfort that I had received after Ken's accident. I also realized that I would need to put fear in its place. It had held me captive for so long. I had lived such a self-focused life because I was fearful of not having enough, not being accepted, and I feared failure.

To reach my goals, I would need to change my mindset. I would need to see myself in the same manner that God saw me. As a man thinketh, so is he! My first step towards success would be to change the way that I thought. My journey to freedom began as I let go of worldly affirmation. Possessions, titles, education, etc., no longer defined me. God began to teach me that as His daughter, I would have everything that I needed. Since He lives inside of me, everything that I need will come.

Seek ye first the kingdom of righteousness, and all these things shall be added unto you. – Matthew 6:33

I had a new understanding of what that scripture meant. I would no longer need to strive for success or worry about what others thought of me. I am designed according to His divine purpose for my life. I am equipped for every good work. I am a gift to the world. My light shines so that others can see. My affirmation comes from Him. For many years, I lived life as if I oversaw it. My life is now completely His and He directs my path.

My hope is that you will discover your path to courage. Perhaps it will be in a common everyday circumstance. Or maybe your journey will be more like mines. God can take a tragic moment of life and redesign it so that it makes you strong, brave, and determined to live life to the fullest and for His glory!

It has been thirteen years since Ken's death. A lot has changed. I have learned that my calling in life is to connect people to resources, people to people, and most importantly - people to God. I now use my life to serve others by way of community and church service. I help nonprofits grow and develop plans and strategies to impact their local community. I am the founder of **UnCommon Courage**, created to inspire and equip women to find, embrace, and connect with their unique voice and purpose with confidence.

Tiffany D Bell

Author Bio

With the definition of professionalism lingering amongst the uncertainty of a trendy culture; Tiffany D Bell stands as proof, that business reliability is far from being a *lost art*, in this generation.

Combining unequivocal poise and diligence with a natural refinement, Tiffany is known best, for her exemplary leadership, compassion, and an unyielding ability to balance cultural demand with a professional vernacular; unmatched by most.

Tiffany D. Bell is a multidimensional leader, influencer, and communal advocate. Having spent more than two decades providing the best in managerial, administrative, and servant leadership, Tiffany is often counted as one able to execute at high levels; regardless of unforeseen circumstances, quintessential business pivots, or various setbacks.

As the Executive Director of the Women's Resource Center of Gulfport, MS; Tiffany encourages women to make positive life choices. Connecting her faith in God with an innate ability for servant leadership, she walks out an intentional effort to impact the lives of young women with the hope of the Gospel. As one on a mission to show them how to step forward in their power when faced with difficult circumstances, Tiffany has translated 25 years of experience in community outreach and leadership training into a formidable blueprint transforming young women's lives.

She is co-director of Success Women's Conference, which was recently named a Top 10 Conference for Professional Women by Essence Magazine. Held annually in September, women from all over the world flood the MS Gulf Coast to be inspired, connected, empowered, and recharged by internationally known speakers and coaches. Attendees leave the conference with a greater sense of confidence and elevated in all areas of life, both professionally and in their personal lives.

Tiffany also has a strong respect for higher education, as she earned her degree in Radiological Health Services in 1998 and has since, given many professional years to its vocation.

The trademark of leadership is an appropriate repute of Tiffany D Bell; as she is also an Honorary Commander for Keesler Air Force Base 2nd Air Force, 81st Medical Group. Having displayed a sensory for communal leadership, she served as a director of Keesler Air Force Protestant Women Group and Bible Study leader for many years, believing that veterans, like herself; tend to flourish naturally when surrounded by community involvement.

Tiffany has also served as the Co-Chairman on the Board of Trustees for Lighthouse Business and Professional Women, a director for the Biloxi Bay Area Chamber, and programs chair for the 2019-2020 year of the Kiwanis Club of Orange Groove, of which she was recently nominated for Lay Person of the

Year. She received the 2019 Tom Tandler Lifetime Achievement Award.

When Tiffany D. Bell is not out serving her community; changing lives throughout Mississippi and abroad, she is a proud mother of two sons, and a grandmother with a firm belief in creating a legacy for her children and grandchildren for years to come.

Tiffany D. Bell.
Leader. Advocate. World-Class Professional.

Let's connect!

FB - https://www.facebook.com/Tiff.D.Bell
IG - https://www.instagram.com/tiffanydbell/?hl=en
IG - https://www.instagram.com/uncommon_courage/?hl=en
Twitter - https://twitter.com/tiffanydbell?lang=en
Linkedin - https://www.linkedin.com/in/tiffany-d-bell-98497262/
Website - https://www.uncommoncourage.cc/
Website - https://www.mynonprofitpro.com/

Girl Get Your Life Together

~ **Dr. Shelia Rivers, DSW, LCSW, MPH**

I knew I had no more to give of myself; no more to give my children and no more to give to my job. I couldn't bring myself to ask anyone for help, even God. All I felt was deep pain and sadness, and I was exhausted. I was exhausted from always having to be strong. I was exhausted from people *telling* me to be strong. As if the reality of my life didn't remind me every single day that I *had* to be strong. If I wasn't, my whole world would come crashing down. It seemed as though the world, and everyone in it, would not let me be anything *but* strong.

The problem is that "being strong" can be a prison when it's the only choice you have. It teaches you that you can't feel weakness and insecurity; you aren't allowed to. "Being strong" taught me, and countless other women, to hide our true emotions. It has taught us that it is not ok to cry in situations where tears are absolutely appropriate. It has taught us to keep the dysfunctions in our family hidden. It has taught us how to push through dysfunction and trauma, leading to unhealthy coping mechanisms. And "being strong" has taught us to disconnect emotionally and insulate ourselves from the outside world instead of seeking help. The world says we need to apply strength to every obstacle. But what we usually need is courage.

The year was 2006. I had recently escaped from an emotionally and psychologically abusive relationship that had absolutely destroyed me. I found myself, once again, in the all too familiar position of being the sole provider for our household. I was stretched thin and all alone. Money was tight, happiness was nowhere to be found. Depression set in and I started failing my classes. I spiraled completely out of control and decided I might as well quit my job too. What the h***? ROCK BOTTOM!

Up until that point, it seemed as if the world would not allow me to be anything other than strong and I felt trapped, controlled, and powerless. As strange as it sounds, giving up was the only way to regain my freedom. My prison had made me feel paralyzed and unsure of everything. But not being strong at least meant that I was back in control of my life; whatever was left of it.

But then a funny thing happened. A voice inside just kept telling me I was not being my true self; that I needed to step outside of my own dysfunction. "**Girl, get your life together,**" the voice said. I was tired of hearing myself complain. I was tired of hearing myself blame others. I was tired of being tired! So, I started seeing a therapist. Then, I met a few women at school who (surprise, surprise) had also hit rock bottom before, and I slowly started building my tribe.

That process of healing was honestly an 'out of body' experience. I had, somehow, stepped outside of my own dysfunctional self and started a journey towards recovery. I wasn't always sure what to do or how to do it, but girl, I was on the road to getting my life together. I had no plan or road map. I just knew I needed to learn to try new things and not be afraid to live. I also needed to learn to be as vulnerable as I was courageous; as willing to lean on my tribe for help as I was to stand on my own. I needed to learn how to embrace my emotionality and femininity, and not let the world define who I was and wasn't allowed to be. In this way, I discovered that there is a difference between strength and courage. ***Strength gives you the shoulders to carry heavy burdens, but courage gives you the heart to overcome them.***
4

The world told me I needed to be strong. The world told me to just lean in and push that rock up that hill until you die. We all have our "lot in life," right? Struggle through this world and God will reward you in the next. That is what we're told. But that voice inside of me was telling me I wasn't being my true self because I was defining myself by my ability to muster up the strength to push through difficult situations. But who I was, my true self, was a woman of courage; someone who would not be satisfied with the "lot" the world wanted to give me. "No sir. Y'all can keep pushing that stone, but I'm getting a backhoe...and then I'm taking a cruise."

One thing I discovered during that time (a time of consistent therapy), is that my favorite part of the process is self-discovery and self-improvement. It was infectious, once I committed myself to doing it. Working to improve my mental and physical health became a regular part of my life. I've embraced the part of me that always strives to think outside of the box, to read something new, and to make connections with people who challenge me in positive ways. And that tribe of women? Unwavering supporters! Heroes in heels!

Don't get me wrong, therapists are indescribably important for providing us with a roadmap. They help us figure out where to go, which route to take, and what kind of car we need to get us there. But your tribe are the ones who come out at 3 am to help you change a flat and get you back on the road. You really do need both, if you're going to make it. It takes courage, not strength, to start the journey. And it takes courage to know when it is time to ask for help.

Finding a soulful purpose is indescribable. There are no words in my tiny vocabulary that can describe how it feels to find a meaningful soulful purpose. It is kind of like finding love; when you find it, you know. And don't worry if your journey doesn't look like everyone else's. Your "rock bottom" may not be as rocky as mine was. Your road to recovery may not be as long either. But you'll know the journey is right for you because it will be rooted in courage, not strength.

Girl Get Your Life Together
Each time I say it something else reveals itself, for the better
Girl Get Your Life Together
It's starting to sound like an affirmation or something like that.
The more I say it the more it becomes my reality
Girl Get Your Life Together
I think I'm starting to love the skin I'm in. Wow, look what a little challenge will do.
Girl Get Your Life Together
Where did all this positive energy come from?
Girl Get Your Life Together
This is how she was born.
Girl Get Your Life Together

Dr. Shelia Rivers

Author Bio

I'm Dr. Shelia Rivers, DSW, LCSW, MPH trauma expert for women. I have been a mental health professional for 13 years. I wear numerous professional hats, such as being the CEO and Chief Therapist of Rivers Psychotherapy Services, published author, Adjunct Professor at Tulane University, Public Speaker, Expert Mental Health Consultant, Social Work Intern Supervisor, and Licensed Clinical Social Worker. I'm presently a Licensed Clinical Social Worker in the surrounding tri-state area - State of Mississippi, the State of Alabama, and the State of Louisiana. I provide counseling services for individuals, children and adolescents, adults, couples, families, and groups.

I am the founder of the holistic wellness program, Girl Get Your Life Together. This program provides a supportive psychoeducational environment for women to discuss sensitive issues related to experiencing and coping with stress, learn more about mental health disorders, address emotional issues, and challenge unhealthy coping skills. Girl Get Your Life Together program is built on the 8 dimensions of wellness: emotional, soul, body, finance, environmental, occupational, social, and intellectual. I am also the author of "She Is," "The Power of Hope," and contributing author of "Unboxed."

In 2020, I was invited to serve as a Board Advisory Member for Unite Empowerment in New Orleans, Louisiana. In 2019, I was a speaker at the Success Women's Conference. In 2019, I was also nominated for

"Most Successful Black Owned Small Business and Most Successful Mental Health Provider." In 2018, I was presented with an award as a Success Woman Influence Leader on the Mississippi Gulf Coast. Over the years, I have been involved with numerous organizations supporting the gift of Helps.

My academic preparation includes Doctor of Social Work from Tulane University, a Masters in Public Health with Healthcare Executive Management, Masters in Social Work, and Bachelors in Psychology. My education provides me with a broad and coherent knowledge of health care policy and executive administration, social and human services, and general psychology along with insight into the cognitive and affective processes that underlie individual human development and behavior. Additionally, it has provided me with greater skills in critical thinking, communication, and collaboration and information utilization.

Through my experience, I have demonstrated my ability to provide consultation to teachers, families, and administrators; complete comprehensive psychological evaluations of adults, children, and adolescents who present with social, emotional, academic, and behavioral difficulties; and in providing direct counseling and intervention to adult, children and adolescents. My areas of concentration consist of strength perspective, empowering and emotionally supporting women and their families, trauma survivors, and program evaluations.

I am versed in evaluating the outcomes of services to ensure their effectiveness. Overall, my background reflects my ability to lead and maintain a strong commitment to professional standards. I am passionate about my gifted path and make a conscious effort to provide an opportunity for growth throughout my journey. I am forever "Empowered to Make a Difference."

I AM Enough!

~ **Ashley Hudson**

Insecurity is a curious drug. It does not envelop you with grand gestures and promises of an escape from a life of stress. No. Insecurity seduces you with your own thoughts. It is a broken record of misplaced personal judgments. A video reel of untruths that plays in your mind the moment you decide to step out on faith.

I was raised in a home where "can't" was considered a swear word. My siblings and I were poured into and nurtured in a way many envied. My parents poured their sweat, love, and energy into raising us with courage, compassion, and confidence. We were given the space to see the world through the eyes of curiosity and wonder instead of fear. I was always reminded that there was nothing that I couldn't do if I put my mind to it.

In so many ways, I excelled in this. I achieved the dreams that I spoke of as a little girl. I became a dentist, a prosthodontist, and a military officer. I thrived on these accomplishments and the accolades that I received from them. From the outside, my life was perfect, and yet there were empty places in my heart that had been shaped by life experiences and society-imposed truths. These had rooted themselves deep into my understanding of myself. The world saw me as a confident, independent woman, while I saw myself as a fraud who would never be enough. The inconsistency in perception came because regardless of what accolade I received, I could never capture the one thing that I longed for the most, a family of my own. In many ways, I coveted this dream of a family. I obsessed about it. I centered my focus around it and found myself in many unequally yoked relationships because of it.

Each time one of the relationships failed, my insecurities would grow. The lies that lived in the edges of my mind would whisper, "See, you aren't good enough"; "You aren't pretty enough"; "You will always be alone." Every broken heart led me further into the belief that I was unwanted and unlovable.
Instead of seeking and accepting the truth of who I was created to be and my identity in Christ, I spent most of my energy striving for perfection. I exhausted all my strength, trying to fit the picture of what was acceptable to society. The fear of my scars and past being revealed and of abandonment kept me disconnected- distanced from loved ones who wanted to pour into my life. I placed my validation squarely in

my ability, achievement, and acceptance from other people, and people are fickle. There is no wonder why my heart was filled with an insecurity that sought to steal my purpose.

I knew I couldn't live this way forever; I was raised to believe that I could do anything, and nothing was out of my grasp. I had to learn to let go of my expectations for a relationship in the time frame I desired, but I wasn't sure how.

The final straw came in the fall of 2015, and it came in the form of a great relationship that suddenly fell apart. We seemed compatible in every way. He was establishing himself as a leader in the community, and he was choosing me! I felt as if I had finally found someone who I could achieve greatness with. It seemed that we were on the road to "Power Couple" status. The perfection was intoxicating. So the sudden ending due to incompatible desires was a gut punch. I'd had my heart broken before, but this one cut to my core. It broke something in me and left a raw vulnerability that I struggled to pinpoint. Yes, I was witnessing another failed relationship and broken heart. I was staring at the abyss of brokenness and the sting of rejection. There was another feeling that seemed to be stronger than the others. It almost felt

You see, for most of my dating life, I had strived to be the perfect girlfriend, the ideal woman. I sought to prove myself and to show that I was worth being chosen. With every new rejection, I became more determined to be seen in the light of perfection I thought others desired. I realized that in all of those relationships, I had been exactly who I thought I SHOULD be, and that wasn't enough.

This was the realization that broke me; I was devastated. However, the beauty in this is that with God, a Masterpiece can be created through devastation. In my case, God had given me an earthly example to reflect my relationship with Him. During this time of brokenness, I was invited to a small group through the church I attended. Within the safety of this group, God began to reveal to me that I was not only striving for perfection and being inauthentic with man, but I was also acting that way in my relationship with Him. My insecurities were a side effect of this misplaced need for perfection. Instead of pressing into the Lord and allowing Him to write my story and show me who I was in Him, I chose my own paths. I then was left feeling as if I had already done too much to be truly used by God. I felt that my past was too murky, and everything bad that happened to me was well deserved. While I believed in God, I had accepted Jesus as my Lord and Savior - I still felt bound to the things of the world. I felt like it was too late for Him to do anything with me. I then projected my human feelings of guilt, shame, and condemnation on a God who only saw me through the eyes of Grace.

It was this Grace that saved me. It was His Grace that allowed me to open up about my past and confess to the women in my small group. It was His Grace that restored my heart and gave me the capacity to learn more about myself and to see myself as He had always seen me. It was His Grace that gave me the peace to wait for the relationship that He had already begun preparing for me.

It is this Grace that keeps me now!

After releasing the expectations that I was striving to attain and shedding those for the purpose that God planned for my life, life shifted in the most beautiful and miraculous way. I gave up seeking the perfect husband and molding myself to be the "perfect" mate. Instead, I found my passion for the elderly. I sought out an opportunity to serve a community that was dear to my heart and I was able to found Wrapped in Love, an organization that helps provide homemade holiday gifts for the nursing home residents.

My newfound freedom from seeking and being also allowed me the space to start another passion project, Undoubted Grace, which allowed me to encourage other women in many phases of life to walk in their purpose and to shed the insecurities that keep them from being their authentic self.

The beautiful gift that came out my focus on the things that God had been asking me to do all along was that God was shaping and molding me into the woman I was always meant to be, and that woman caught the eye of the man who is now my husband. He was drawn to everything that made me imperfect, and my relentless pursuit to be exactly who I was meant to be.

Insecurity nearly broke me. It kept me striving to be perfect in a role I was never meant to play. Authenticity has allowed me the freedom to excel at everything that was meant to be. The road wasn't easy, and while today I can share a more authentic me with others, insecurities still try to infiltrate my heart. I simply remember three truths that combat the insecurity: I am shielded, protected, and covered by the truth of God's word; I am loved and cherished by the Creator of the Universe; I am a daughter of the King, made in His image, and heir to the inheritance of heaven.

I am enough!

Dr. Ashley Hudson

Author Bio

Award-winning dentist, speaker, blogger, and working mother self-care coach with a passion for seeing women walk in authenticity and God-given purpose! Dr. Ashley Harris Hudson truly epitomizes what is to be The Standard of Excellence.

Ashley graduated from Hampton University in 2007 with a bachelor's degree in Chemistry. She went on to UNC Chapel Hill to obtain her Doctorate in Dentistry and later obtained a Biomedical Sciences Master's degree, specializing in Prosthodontics. While obtaining her graduate degrees and completing her residency, Ashley has also served our country as a proud member of the United States Air Force.

Currently living in Alaska, her time in the Air Force continues to move her and her family around the country. Nonetheless, wherever she's lived, she has always left her mark. Some examples of this include:
- ✓ Mentoring a new generation of minority dental students;
- ✓ Founding a non-profit organization, Corinthians 13, that serves our often-underserved elderly population;
- ✓ Leading an international network of Christian Women Bloggers, designed to equip one another with the tools needed to inspire and encourage growth

Even with these accomplishments, Ashley felt the need to pour into a segment of the population that she, herself, often felt neglected in. This passion for encouraging others led to the founding of **Undoubted Grace**, an online community of working moms and busy professional women learning to enjoy and embrace their individual stories of womanhood. She coaches overwhelmed women in balancing work and family life, practicing intentional self-care, and cultivating spiritual growth.

Ashley's guiding principle in life is inspired by Psalm 121:1-2, *"I lift up my eyes to the mountains—where does my help come from? My help comes from the Lord, the Maker of heaven and earth."* Using the firm foundation instilled in her from childhood as a guide, Ashley spends most of her time learning in her most rewarding mission, creating a nurturing Christ-centered home for her family.

Do It Afraid

~ Dr. Aimee Clute

Have you ever been at a place in your life where you wanted more? Everything was good, but something was driving you for greater. That's what happened to me.

I had grown up as a preacher's kid, traveling across the U.S. ministering in music with my family. Some of my earliest memories included tent meetings, camp meetings, choirs singing, and watching people's lives being changed. Even as a teenager, my dates consisted of going to revival services, and then to the pizza parlor afterward. I went on to marry a preacher. For over 30 years, we had traveled preaching the gospel and ministering in song, all the while pastoring a church on the gulf coast. Ministry has always been a part of my life.

As I grew in my relationship with God and in my faith, there always seemed to be a constant desire to do more. I was intrigued by great revivalists, such as Aimee Semple Mcpherson, Kathryn Kuhlman, Smith Wigglesworth, A. A. Allen, Jack Coe, and Lester Sumrall to name a few. The more I studied their ministries, the more I knew I wanted what they had: a healing ministry with the ability to reach the masses for the kingdom.

One day, while in prayer and fasting, I received a message from a young pastor in Pakistan. In times past, I had been hesitant about returning certain messages, due to so many scams. But in this case, I knew the Holy Spirit was drawing me to respond. Who knew this pastor and wife would become so dear to me? Soon, I would begin to minister to the people of Pakistan. I'm so thankful for today's technology. Translated videos were taken to many small villages, and within a short time, hundreds of people came to know the Lord. The response of the people was overwhelming.

My husband and I began to prepare for our first trip to the Middle East when he became seriously ill. Doctors would no longer release him to travel, leaving me to make a very serious decision: would I make this trip alone? Pakistan is a 97% Muslim country. It was at this time, Christians were under severe persecution. Many were being killed or imprisoned for their faith. Women are taught to submit and remain silent. This was a huge decision to make. I had never been out of the country without my husband, but after much prayer and my husband's blessing, I knew that one member of our staff and I would go to Pakistan.

This would be my very first crusade. My heart became full as I stepped out onto the stage, overlooking the thousands of people in attendance. I knew I was made for this! High walls and buildings surrounded the property where the crusade was being held. I could see soldiers all around, carrying assault rifles, and observing everything going on. It was then that the Holy Spirit warned me to be mindful of all things at all times, but not to let fear overtake me. Because fear would lead to my death. I was later informed that we were in the area in which the Taliban trained their soldiers

I will never forget that night, as I preached about Ezekiel in the valley of dry bones and I sang the song "Break Every Chain." Thousands received the Lord Jesus as their savior. Many were healed and set free. When I left the meeting, I sat in the car and wept. Not only would their lives be changed, but mine as well.

My trip consisted of a revival service for pastors and leaders, a major crusade in the city, preaching in several of the villages, handing out Bibles in the Urdu language, and performing a baptismal service in a natural well. I was the second woman to evangelize in the country of Pakistan, leading 23,000 souls to Christ. There was nothing more gratifying than knowing I had done what God called me to do.

Days following my return home were difficult. For ten days, I had experienced life in unsanitary conditions, no electricity, and temperatures rising up to 120 degrees. I had seen people living in caves. So many comforts of life, I had taken for granted. God began to show me how He had kept and protected me. I had done what so many others would not have dared to do.

Soon after my return from Pakistan, I would begin an in-depth study on the book of Esther: the story of an orphan girl, a mere victim of circumstance. She was beautiful, yet so broken, but God saw what she could be. He put her in a place where she could find healing;

all the while, He was drawing out the GREATNESS within her. She went from a commonplace to a place of royalty. She could've become comfortable in her position. Why, she'd finally made it! Designer gowns, red bottom shoes, and all, but she decided to step out of the box, even though it would be risky. She'd been placed in a position of political influence that would lead to the saving of a nation.

This story spoke to me. Every little girl desires to be a princess or a queen, but so many are broken. Women have so much power within. They are the very creatures God used to bring forth new life. Deep inside, I felt the Holy Spirit was telling me that he was going to begin to use women in a greater capacity and raise modern-day Esthers. But in order for many to move into their place of greatness, they would need to find healing first. So, I began a women's retreat. A place where they could find healing, learn to not only believe in themselves but the God within them, and to learn that they too can make a difference.

Soon, I was asked to speak for a women's conference, on the Book of Esther, in the state of Oklahoma. As I was traveling to the meeting, I had car trouble. Immediately after I pulled off to the side of the road, in the middle of nowhere, a highway patrolman appeared. He promised he wouldn't leave me until I was safe. He seemed to be a very peculiar man, introducing himself as St. Patrick. I felt very uneasy while waiting for a tow truck. I then received a call from a dear friend in Mississippi who was also a highway patrolman. My friend spoke to the officer that was waiting with me and assured me that I was in good hands.

After what seemed like forever and several conversations later, St. Patrick began to give me instructions on something I had been praying and fasting about. Only God knew about it. I knew it was my next assignment, and that was to begin to fight for religious freedoms.

A couple of days later, I found out that my highway patrol friend had tried to contact St. Patrick, having his badge and jurisdiction numbers, only to find out that St. Patrick did not exist. It was at this point that I knew a messenger from heaven had been sent to me. Or as some would say, I had entertained an angel unaware.

As I look back at these turn of events, I can see God's hand upon my life. Everything that I have gone through or have experienced, was God preparing me for my greater. God used Pakistan to teach me faith over fear, or some might say, uncommon courage.

When I think about God taking this Mississippi girl and using me in a less privileged country like Pakistan, yet having such great results, I think, "What could God do with me in the good ole U.S. of A.?" A place where we have freedom, but yet those freedoms are being challenged each and every day. Then I think about Esther, who had gone from being an orphan girl to a queen, yet she chose to put her life on the line for the sake of others.

Many times, we look at the situations we face and think it's all about us, but I choose to look at the bigger picture. We all have a story to tell, but for God to use Esther at her greatest potential, she had to realize it wasn't about herself. There was more to her purpose! Then there was St Patrick. You see I'd prayed and asked God for very specific instructions for my next. I'd made some mistakes along the way and I didn't want to mess up again. My timing needed to line up with God's timing, in order to fulfill His will for my life. Just to think of how God thought enough about me to send an angel to speak to me meant more than I could express. And now the rest was up to me.

It doesn't matter your position, your age, or your financial status. From the common housewife to the CEO of a major corporation, from a college student to a senior citizen, or maybe the mayor of your town to a lobbyist of the Supreme Court, there is always room for the greater! Delay is not denial; rejection is not final.

What is crazy? It's the act of doing the same thing over and over and expecting different results.

What is courage? It's the quality shown by someone who decides to do something difficult or dangerous, even though they may be afraid. Each of the events I described in this chapter has played such an important role. Trust me when I say, I've been pulled out of my comfort zone. But because God's hand has been on this, I know I was made for this.

With the recent election and in such times of uncertainty, we need leaders, men and women alike, who are willing to take a stand no matter what they've gone through or what's been said about them, to go the extra mile. With God in control, there are no limits! You have a purpose to fulfill! As one person once told me, "Do it afraid!" You can make a difference.

Dr. Aimee Clute

Author Bio

Dr. Aimee Clute celebrates forty years of full-time ministry, holding a doctorate in Divinity and a certificate of Chaplaincy. Dr. Aimee is celebrating twenty-nine years of marriage to Apostle Thomas Clute having two sons, one daughter, and two grandchildren. Apostle and Dr. Clute have pastored the "River of Life Church" in Gulfport, Mississippi for twenty-eight years.

Dr. Aimee has appeared on television broadcasts and has had the privilege of ministering in grand arenas before persons of great political influence, as well as, alongside prominent ministers and artists. Dr. Clute has traveled throughout the United States and abroad to nine other countries for ministry in word and song. 23,000 souls were led to the Lord in Pakistan alone.

2017 and 2018 recipient of the Gulf Coast Gospel Music Awards. Performed recently to 40,000 people at Lakewood Church in Houston, Texas.

But God!

~ **Sonya Smith**

We have all heard the saying, "When life throws you lemons make lemonade." Such a profound statement to encourage a positive "I can do all things" attitude during adversity and hardship. I must have made gallons of lemonade throughout my spiritual journey. Some sour, some bitter, and my best lemonade by far has been sweet and refreshing to the pallet of my life. All of life's flavors have contributed to helping me become a better stronger and courageous woman of God. Throughout my journey, I have learned life is truly what you make it to be and we get to be participants in creating and choosing the life we desire. We get to choose courage over fear, unspeakable joy over discouragement, and letting go over holding on. No matter how we view our lives and experiences, we get to choose our reality.

Choosing courage in the midst of a dark and hopeless reality takes strength from the Lord. It takes perseverance, faith, and an unstoppable will and dependency on God. Is possessing courage easy? No. Is it possible to attain? Yes. There is a risk that you will need to take, and it will cost you something, but you will be stronger and better on the other side for it. Now, you may be saying to yourself, "It's just too hard, there is no way I can take this step of faith." My brother and sister, do not allow fear to cripple you and rob you from receiving God's best.

When Jesus told Peter to step out of the boat and walk on water towards Him, Peter's faith in the Lord gave him the courage to get out of the boat. It was only until Peter took his eyes off Jesus and turned his focus on the storm that he began to sink (Matthew 14:22-33). Our Faith in God activates our courage. It strengthens us to be brave and step out of the boat because we know the "One" Who is walking with us and for us. Through the storms of life, great sufferings we will encounter. But it is during these times when we must choose to be courageous despite the odds against us.

As a native of Brooklyn, New York, the concrete jungle taught me a lot about courage. Courage and perseverance were something the streets taught you and I was determined to soak it all in even if it cost me my life. Although I grew up going to church frequently, I did not have a relationship with God. I knew God as an acquaintance, a distant relative. Many of the courageous choices that I thought were wise were foolish. I was being brave about things that were trying to kill me and determined to be rebellious, even when I knew what I was doing was wrong.

From drugs and alcohol, living in a drug house, widowed, abusive relationships, divorced, you name it, I left no sinful stone unturned. My life, for many years, was spiraling out of control and no one or nothing could stop me. The many trials and tribulations in my life caused me to feel defeated, rejected, and abandoned. I had no self-love and I self-medicated by looking for love in all the wrong places. I knew better, but I chose not to do better. But I always knew in my heart God desired more from me; however, I felt unworthy to be used by God and I certainly felt like God would never forgive me for all the wrong things I had done.

As a child, I would make up so many stories about everything; I guess I was fantasizing about what I wish I could have and be. I continued this behavior pattern most of my life, even up to my adulthood, stretching the truth, manipulating, and lying about everything. As I reflect on those times, I realize, I was just a child crying out for attention. A child that was longing to be heard, loved, and understood. I was always vocal, speaking up and speaking out when I saw things that were not right. My spirit was never satisfied with just being ordinary. I always dreamed of doing and being somebody that would help change this world for the better.

My father was the first man to lie and break my heart. His absence brought on emotional disorders that stemmed from issues of trust, lack of self-esteem, and identity issues that led to repeated cycles of dysfunctional decisions in relationships with men. My father's absence in my life, especially during my youth and adolescent years, was ultimately the root to all my trauma and hurt, but I could no longer blame or hold him hostage in my heart. I had to choose to forgive him and forgive myself so that I could move forward in my life.

I met my oldest daughter's father, Rudolph at the age of sixteen years old, lost my virginity, became pregnant, and miscarried all by the age of seventeen. I felt so alone and afraid. I felt as though I disappointed my mother because of my bad choices. My mother is one of the most courageous people I know. She gave birth to me at the age of seventeen, raised my siblings, and taught me to love and fear the Lord. I remember facing my mother with such shame and disgust for what I had done. If only I could turn back time, I would have done things differently, I would have listened to my mother's advice about preserving my body and loving myself. My mother's response was one I certainly did not expect. She did not yell at me. She extended grace and compassion towards me. I left our conversation feeling loved and affirmed. My mother has always been a source of courage and strength for my siblings and me.

At the age of twenty, Rudolph and I married, and he was murdered two years later. I was also seven months pregnant with our daughter, Rudy. Becoming a widow and single mother at the age of twenty-two is by far indescribable. My heart was crushed and what made it worse was no one was brought to justice for killing my husband. Everything inside of me wanted to give up after losing the love of my life. I thought about committing suicide and even attempted, but God intervened and had my sister call and invite me to her church revival. She begged me to come to church that night and God granted me enough strength to walk through those church doors and His presence met me at the altar. Glorious Temple Church of God and Christ is where I grew up, but strayed away because I wanted to live life on my terms, but God's call on your life is irrevocable. The Lord allured me back to the place where I gave my heart to Him. I rededicated my life back to Christ that evening and began the road to healing, wholeness, and restoration with Jesus.

As I continued my spiritual journey throughout the years, I had some bumps in the roads; much of it had to do with the open wounds of rejection and abandonment that still was haunting me from my fatherless childhood. Even after all I had gone through and all the Lord had delivered me from, I was still searching for love. I know that sounds crazy. You think I would have learned my lesson. It was the thorn in my side that almost took my life. I met and married after six months of us courting a charming, handsome man that I thought was sent by God. I later learned it was set-up by the enemy. After the happily ever after wedding, the real him appeared, or maybe he was always there, but I was too blind to see it. He became verbally, physically, and emotionally abusive and for six years I stayed with a man that dishonored me as his wife and God's precious daughter, because I wanted so desperately to save my marriage. What was

I doing wrong? How could I make him love me and not abuse and cheat on me? These were all the questions that tormented me daily. There were no signs of abuse in his tone or actions during our period of dating. He was just as charming, loving, and caring as one could be, but looking back, I realize I saw what he wanted me to see in him, and what I wanted to see in him was the potential of someone loving me for me. This was a bad choice. I became a victim of domestic violence, but God gave me faith - small as a mustard seed and the strength of lionesses - to leave and defeat this abusive cycle of my life for good. The Lord again made a way of escape for me and I never looked back. The Lord heard and answered my prayers, the prayers of my mother, family friends, and loved ones. I was finally FREE.

Everyone will face seasons of famine, trials, and tribulations. The biggest mistake we can make during these times is believing that we are inadequate for the task. God would surely get you through it. Even if you have to crawl, cry and lose people that you thought would be there for you, take the step of faith and move forward. You are a carrier of God's glory. When you move, God will move. He is already working it out for your good.

God never gave up on me. He showed me through His unfailing love that I am more than enough, and I can be used by Him. Everything, the Lord allows us to go through will not be wasted. Our Creator knows, hears, and sees all things. His perfect will is unchanging and everything we experience in life - good and bad - God can, and will use to bring glory and honor to His Name. It takes courage and strength to overcome the odds that are stacked up against you, but it is not over until God says it is over.

"For such a time as this," is the scripture verse I lean on for courage (Esther 4:14). Queen Esther's courage to save her people from death, even if it meant her own life, taught me that courage leans hard on God's strength. If we desire to possess courage, we must remember we are a child of God. Trust and obey the Lord and walk in His strength and wisdom.

I have no regrets in my life, only gratitude. Shame, guilt, and condemnation no longer consume me. I am no longer searching for love in all the wrong places because I found unconditional love in Jesus. I have gained more than I have lost from my past experiences; unmerited favor, grace, a closer walk with Jesus, and courage that can move mountains. I count it all joy to have been afflicted, for my afflictions were only temporary, but the treasures that I am storing up in Heaven are for eternity. My two beautiful daughters are my greatest gifts. My full-time service to ministry as a Pastor and making disciples for Christ is by far the most courageous thing I have ever done in my life.

Sonya Smith

Author Bio

The true funnel toward effective leadership is service. Embodying that preface with the highest of honor; is servant leader, Sonya Smith.

Sonya Smith is an International Best-Selling Author, Speaker, Lieutenant, and Pastoral advocate for the Salvation Army Mobile County Corps of Mobile, AL.

Her altruism reputes her as one, known for placing the causes of others, above her own. With both social disparity and various forms of injustice towards humanity as her leading passions; Sonya is often a featured speaker on diverse platforms for her devout advocacy.

Sonya's motto is clear: when we tolerate injustice on any level, we are choosing to be comfortable and complex; at the expense of innocent lives, who are suffering by the hands of the oppressor.

Making the most of every opportunity to serve others, Sonya Smith brings a sense of community to every project, mission, and event. One of her most memorable accomplishments was in leading a renovation project with the Salvation Army. There, she led the total reconstruction of a house owned by the organization; transforming it into a "Community Engagement Center".

The project was so successful, that in January of 2020, Sonya was able to dedicate the center back to the local community; repurposed, as a communal staple for unity and fellowship amongst its inhabitants.

To accompany a dedicated career in service-oriented leadership, Sonya has displayed a great respect for education and ordinance. She owns a degree in Practical Ministry, and is both a commissioned and ordained minister and pastor; receiving her license from The Salvation Army Evangeline Booth Seminary School; Officers Commission. A celebrated leader, Sonya Smith is the humble recipient of: the Lt. Colonel Israel L. and Eva D. Gathier Award, The Warrior Spirit of Evangelism Award, and holds a Certificate of Appreciation Award for Hurricane Michael Disaster Relief Service.

Invoked sincerely, by a sheer faith in God and the wellbeing of mankind, Sonya submits that love; is her primary inspiration. Believing it to be both, a repellent against hated and the only force credible; in bringing transformation to the world.

Sonya Smith.

Leader. Advocate. Global Servant.

The Patient

~ Shadaria Allison

Tear-stained eyes crowded the front of my face as I desperately asked God for help.

My late twenties were stained with resentment and the vivid reminders of a life survived, yet seldom lived. Divorce, dead-end jobs, toxic relationships, and the loss of a child would be my final straw before I gave in to the acknowledgment that something about the way I reasoned had to change. It would be in that moment of prayer that I would find an unconventional response from God.

"Go to the Doctor."

Mental illness had been one of the most resisted realities I'd seen growing up in the black community; yet at the ripe age of 27, through the avenue of prayer, I was diagnosed with adult ADHD and acute anxiety disorder. After making it through extensive testing and brain simulations, I was called into a small room with a smiling doctor.

"That was easy enough," I said.

"Ms. Allison, my name is Dr. Bullock."

"Nice to meet you," I replied. "I'm sure I passed," I continued. "I answered every question correctly and all the scores came back with a green check."

I paused long enough to see him smile and proceed with my results.

"Ms. Allison," he said, "you see, we don't measure your test scores based on accuracy; we base them on response. Your brain's ability to connect with what is in front of you at a proficient speed is what we use," he continued. "When we measured your brain's ability to respond up against your ability to choose correctly, we found results indicative of someone with ADHD."

Dr. Bullock would go on to describe the relationship patterns, emotional dispositions; even the food choices connected to adult ADHD, and with every explanation, I heard the contents of my prayer found in my diagnosis. I left his office with a prescription and a soul full of questions.

"How could I be a woman of faith, and live with this verdict? They are just trying to diagnose me with ADHD because I'm black!" I said to myself. Pride would not release its grip on my thoughts, no matter how blatant my life's choices screamed back at me.

I was met with an opportunity, in the form of prayer and a doctor's appointment; I could either remain a woman shackled to past failure or a woman committed to whatever it took to change the trajectory of my life. I chose the change.

Today, I am a two-time best-selling author, speaker, and women's advocate with a passion to reform churches into state-of-the-art facilities, in taking the mentally ill, drug-addicted, and homeless individuals. For the last six years, since my diagnosis, I have been able to write over eleven books, most of them geared towards my passion for reform. I am certified in Mental Health Studies and have been featured in newspapers, awarded with nominations from philanthropic giants; such as United Way and Ellis Island Medal of Honors Society. I am the campus officer with Phi Theta Kappa Honor Society and will graduate from college with honors in the spring. I am CEO of a multidimensional business conglomerate servicing beauty, business, and bios under the name of: *Dr. Allison the Beauty Practitioner.*

These accomplishments and many more weren't achieved from my own ability, nor were they attained because I was "God's Favorite." Instead, they are the genuine results of an authentic relationship with both faith and logic, the humility to understand that generational bondage is a choice, and the wisdom in applying sound reason; when issues supersede the false comforts offered in stale religion.

Jesus advised us in the word of God that the church was to be a hospital for the sick. It is then our responsibility, as *walking temples,* to know when to see the doctor in real life.

This generation has been presented with an unequivocal opportunity to change the way we think, while simultaneously processing personal trauma on grave levels.

I stand as a woman committed to lifelong transformation by the renewing of my mind.

I pray that this chapter helps someone believe in God like never before.

I pray that this chapter inspires those struggling with the stigmas placed on people who battle mental illness.

I pray this chapter brings some young woman to her knees in prayer so that she too may encounter God's touch, but most importantly His response

Cheers to having uncommon courage!

Shadaria Allison

Author Bio

Shadaria A. Allison is a best-selling author of 11 books. She is a public speaker, community organizer, influencer, and a rising advocate for women; both young and old. Determined to remain a deliberate investor in the welfare of many, Shadaria commits to being a voice that shifts cultural perspectives, worldwide. Her declaration is simple; she is a woman on a mission and she is, *#married2it.*

Shadaria has graced national platforms such as Fox News, United Way, and the Birmingham Times, all in celebration for her keen ability to connect with people on a universal scale.

Addressing matters from a place of wisdom; her reach isn't limited to business and social influence alone, as Shadaria is a strong advocate for women's issues and the importance of female leadership. She was the first female in the state of Alabama to counteract a derogatory celebrity parade into a reversed processional march in a campaign against the sexual exploitation, trafficking, and promiscuity of women and teen girls in 2018.

Today, she remains an advocate for hundreds of women. Taking on a myriad of social issues surrounding the advancement of women in America and abroad. In 2017, Shadaria petitioned the President of the United States of America to review the Equal Pay Act, in an effort to raise awareness of economic inequality amongst women. She gained over

100 signatures through a mere social media post alone.

Recognized amongst the rising millennial leaders of this generation, Shadaria Allison plans to continue to touch lives. One woman at a time.

A Prison Cell of Fear

~ Hanna Lorraine

Every time it is about to rain, my leg gives off an achy sensation, a reminder of what I went through- what God brought me through. I am now a victorious conqueror. Who would've thought a battle against fear could be waged through a car crash?

I always thought I was living cautious, calculated, and careful.

Every opportunity I let pass by, every unlived moment to step up, or speak up, were just self-preservation skills meant to keep away unwanted outcomes.... or so I thought. A day without embarrassment was a success, and a day without failing at something meant I was safe. What looked like comfort and predictability was a life sentence in a prison cell called fear.

Until one day, I awoke to the sounds of metal crushing and people calling my name. Insert a hospital scene where I'm being rolled here and there, to this test and that xray, and back to one room and later to another. I was informed I suffered a severe concussion, a broken leg, and memory loss. Later, I was told I was resuscitated at the scene of the crash.

Fear was with me as I was hearing all this. It told me, "You need to stay down; you aren't capable. See, what you feared happened. You failed."

Yes, what I feared had happened. I had failed at avoiding a car accident. It took four months to be fully rehabilitated. The accident significantly weakened my memory. It was as if my mind was a non-stick frying pan, with my thoughts sliding off into darkness. Fear latched onto this temporary handicap, drained my courage, and grew stronger as I prepared to drive again.

Driving again- the thought made me nauseous. I begged God not to let it happen. I gave Him very real and valid reasons as to why I should not drive again. Days went by, and it was time for me to start looking at new cars. Some more days went by, and I found myself reluctantly sitting in a car dealership. So I prayed again and waited. "Come on, God make this stop!" I demanded. He did not stop the purchase of a Suzuki Aerio. I froze when the keys were placed into my hands. My dad saw the look on my face, and graciously asked the salesperson if they could drive it home for me. They kindly obliged, and I felt like a failure that I had to inconvenience their day. I could see fear laughing at my awkward situation. Fear had me where it wanted me: too afraid to drive and ashamed of myself for failing, once again, to move out of fear. It was a chess move I could not maneuver out of.

I felt let down that God didn't answer my prayer. I didn't know God was about to answer another prayer. He wasn't going to stop me from driving, but rather, He would help me stop fear from driving my life. Through His Word, He reminded me that if I truly believed where He says I can do all things through Him and that I am more than a conqueror, that means I must accept that fear has been lying to me. I couldn't go through life believing both God and fear. One of them is right, and one of them is wrong. I get to make that decision and whichever I choose determines the quality of life I live and whether I thrive or merely survive. I was tired of hiding to survive, but I was also scared of failing again. What if my next failure is more significant than this last? I asked this question as I stared into His Word, what if next time is worse? Fear of failure had always unknowingly lived with me and only now, through the accident, was its presence revealed. The beautiful thing about "what if" is God knows what is on the other side; it is Himself. He is on the other side catching every outcome with His sovereignty. If I choose to trust God and believe His Word, I can give up wanting a guarantee that it will all work out without another failure. Even if things fall apart and crash again, I can have the courage to view the wreckage as a chance to rebuild instead of a reason to quit. The ability to do all things through Him means that I can have the courage to do hard things, experience failure, and be at peace when "things don't work out." The sting of failure doesn't have to produce poison in me; instead, it is a growing pain used to mature my wisdom and gain experience. That missed opportunity because I lacked the courage to say "yes", the invite that expired on the kitchen counter because I assumed I would be "too awkward", they don't have to happen again. I can be brave and live and go for all of them!

I'll never forget driving myself to another state after the accident. Two hours of driving, two hours of fear not in the driver's seat. Did fear try to hop in before the trip? Yes, and I still felt my breath tighten as I merged onto the highway. But this time, I chose to believe God over fear. I decided to surrender the outcome of the trip to His hands and be okay with what lay ahead. That trip opened up opportunities to me that have forever changed my life for good. The acceleration onto the highway awakened my courage to go for things that seem impossible and to let life unfold with God in control, not fear.

Nowadays, when fear comes around looking for a visit, instead of running to it like an old friend, I get in my car, hit the gas, and drive.

Hanna Lorraine

Author Bio

We live in a society undeniably shaken by cultural restraint, devastation, and traumatic circumstance. Times like these, require individuals born with an awed ability; to serve, aid, and foster the environments necessary, in transforming the lives of many. Graced with that innate ability, is communal leader, Hanna Marmalich.

Hanna Marmalich is an International Best Selling Author, mental health advocate, writer, and overseer at Safe Harbor Clinic; *a thriving Outpatient Mental Health and Addiction Center in Long Beach, Mississippi.* Servicing the entire gulf coast, Safe Harbor Clinic was established in 2016, by Hanna's husband; neuro-psychiatrist, Dustin Marmalich, MD; for the sole purpose of providing the best mental health and addiction treatment to those in need. Staying true to that intent, her husband advised, that Safe Harbor Clinic required nothing short of a world-class facilitator; with a deep compassion for the broken, the unseen, and the forgotten struggles, experienced by his patients. Serving as an undeniable fit, Hanna Marmalich became the lead facilitator and Manager of Safe Harbor Clinic.

Hanna's mantra is simple; *God equips those he calls.*

Operating as one *truly* called, Hanna Marmalich uses her background in practical life redemption, infused with various service projects and platforms; to provide encouragement to the entire world.

One of her favorite ways to exude servant leadership, is through the unyielding influence of social media. Hanna is the curator of **Seasons of Grace by Hanna Lorraine**, a faith-based Instagram page created in congruence with her self-published devotional, to encourage believers in the "thick of life"; to get through difficult times by the power of a flourishing relationship with God. Her inspirational content has touched many, as thousands of online followers engage weekly, in the anticipation of the selfless exhortation provided through Hanna's content.

Showing no plans of slowing down, Hanna Marmalich is committed to the emotional, mental, and spiritual alignment of humanity. From her advocacy of those struggling to find peace in their cognitive health, to providing emotional support to a global audience, it is clear, that Hanna was fashioned; *for such a time as this.*

Hanna Marmalich. Leader. Advocate. Servant.

Life Restarted

~ Liz Hoop

I was born in Jackson, MS, and raised in MS until I left for college in Springfield, MO. I was raised in a Christian home, with my dad becoming a pastor when I was nine years old.

My mom became ill with Hodgkin's disease, so we returned to Brandon, MS, where I graduated from high school. Mom passed away the summer before my senior year. I graduated and went to work for a construction company as their bookkeeper/secretary. It was after this time we had moved to Booneville, MS. Dad had remarried and was back to pastoring. I left home at that time to go to Bible College in Springfield, MO.

While in college, I went to work for a nursing home as a nursing assistant. That's where I got my first experience of working with the elderly. It's also where I saw the sadness of people being dropped off and never visited again. I remember how heartbroken I was for these people.

After two years of college, I left there, married, and lived in Memphis, TN, where that marriage ended in an annulment. I met my second husband there. We married and the next week moved to Houston, TX, where he had accepted a new job, thus causing that move. After a few years of working with a bank, suddenly, I was laid off. That meant looking for a job in a vast city where Compaq Computers (now HP) was located. I was fortunate to get a temporary job assignment with them in 1986. That first week, I was offered a permanent position and began my career there, which lasted for seventeen years. I had survived ten years of layoffs until July 2001. At that time, unemployment was high. Many companies were downsizing. Then it was 9/11! I finally found a part-time job as the webmaster for a junior college and, along with that job, also began a new career path in outside sales. During these seventeen years, once again, I was divorced and remarried.

February 2004, I began a sales position with an office equipment company. In May 2004, my husband came home and said he wasn't happy being married, stating that we were finished being married. I lived a life that had not reflected Christian values from the time I had moved to TN until then.

On a cold call in May of 2004, I met a man who led me back to Jesus right there in his place of business. Don't think I will ever forget this man's name – Wild Bill. Big changes started happening for me then as I was single again, but this time was not getting into a relationship with a man. For the next two years, my family would begin to tell me, especially one sister, that it was time to come home to MS. I fought this because I had a life, friends, and family in Houston and felt moving back to MS. I would be so bored. The only people that I knew were my family and some of their friends.

So now as to the boredom issue... I currently serve as a board of director on several boards here – Mental Health Association of South MS, South Mississippi Special Need Organization, Anchored Hearts Community Resources, Teen Challenge of MS for Women, Adopt A Grandparent Day and am involved in my church and have met so many people.

In September 2006, I loaded up all my belongings, left my family, friends, and, most notably, my adult son, and moved back to MS to begin working for an office equipment company out of Mobile, AL. Because of the divorce, my "love" of shopping and spending, I had amassed quite a bit of debt thanks to credit cards and was struggling financially, so In April 2013, I found myself on the verge of foreclosure of my home.

I filed bankruptcy to get myself back on track and not lose my home. During the bankruptcy period then (April 2013 – April 2018), I learned a couple of valuable lessons. I learned humility, and how to lean on God and have faith to trust Him to take care of me. There were many times between bi-monthly paydays, where I only had between $200 and $300 to make it. I had to pay cash for everything: groceries, gas, and bills, but I never once needed anything because the first thing I always did was pay my tithe on my gross pay. I enjoyed vacations, trips, and dinners out because my Heavenly Provider was watching over me.

A couple of times, too, I received messages that God was going to restore all I had lost during all of this. I had a couple of other jobs after the office equipment company until Feb of 2017, when I began working in the field of hospice. Starting with the new career field in Feb 2017, God fulfilled His promise, and my salary doubled from my previous employer! I thoroughly enjoy working in hospice, as I have such a heart for people and showing the love of Christ to others. In November 2019, when the corporate office of the hospice I was working for announced they were closing our MS office, I knew this didn't surprise God and that all was going to be ok. It was also when my family, one sister, in particular, was going to need me, as her precious husband was leaving this earth after a long battle with cancer.

The week after he passed, I received a text message from Solace Hospice asking to meet with them regarding their position. I had not applied with them nor ever really heard of them but God. He put me with this company that is family-owned by an amazing Christian couple. The mission statement for Solace Hospice is "Caring with compassion and dignity from our family to yours." I know this is where I belong.

I've started over several times in my life, and each move was scary full of unknowns, but I know that anything is possible if I will be an obedient daughter to my Heavenly Father. He guides my steps and places people in my path daily, for which I am eternally grateful!!

Liz Hoop

Author Bio

It has been said that wisdom grows from places of great adversity. Engineered to help others find their way out; is philanthropic liaison, Liz Hoop.

Liz Hoop is an International Best-Selling Author, speaker, communal leader, and tenured liaison with Solace Hospice. Professionalism, being the minimum standard in all she does, Liz attributes the *cause of people*; her greatest trademark. Having served many years at an executive level, in the areas of Marketing and Management; it has been a *common thread* of *people-centric* ethics that has ushered Liz into the vastness of philanthropy, overall.

Liz Hoop currently serves on the board of directors for the Mental Health Association of South Mississippi, Special Needs Organization of South MS, Anchored Hearts Community, Adopt A Grandparent Day, and Teen Challenge for Women in MS; a complete echo of her heart's desire to serve humanity. She is also a great help within the local faith-based community, as Liz serves both; co-leader of a single women's life group and is also an appreciated leader of the women's ministry at The Springs in Hurley, Mississippi.

Liz' motto is simple: Selflessly give your time and best efforts for the betterment of others; on purpose.

Whether it's serving the local community, uplifting members of her faith communal body of members with song, or pouring out unyielding love and support to those in need, Liz Hoop is intentional in creating a life of service; respected both above and on earth.

When Liz is not out; volunteering throughout her local community, she enjoys serving others and spending time with loved ones and close friends.

Liz Hoop. Leader. Motivator. Servant.

Forever Free

~ Lisa Parsons

One of the greatest obstacles in living life courageously is the mindset that we must please other people in order to be "good." What we believe about ourselves and others is the seat of most of our responses and decisions. The drive to please other people creates a vacuum of unmet needs for basic dignity and respect and ensures that we will never reach the God-given potential that we were created for. While thinking we are "keeping peace," we are, in fact, nurturing bitterness and maintaining conflict and hostility.

I was raised to be a people pleaser from the day I was born. No one told me that was my role. No one consciously thought "I will raise this child to please me." The training could be found in the attitude that I was immersed in moment by moment in daily life. I suspect this is true of all of us to some extent. Our cultural expectation is that good parents raise well-behaved children. The assumption is that well-behaved children sit still, look good, perform well, and never disagree with their parents. Some individuals have recognized this attitude as unrealistic, while others try to live up to it and demand the same from those around them. This attitude robs us of individuality, the ability to mature emotionally, and understanding our need for a Savior.

My own story of courage began the day I looked in the mirror and realized that I no longer knew who I was. I had just had another fight with my husband which ended with me finally understanding that no matter how hard I tried, no matter how many self-help books I read and changes I made, no matter how closely I tried to follow what I thought my husband wanted, it would never be enough. I had lived the past 15 years trying to be good enough to prevent his anger, criticism, and derision. I tried to be pretty enough, smart enough, and busy enough. I had submitted my wants and needs to his leadership to the extent that I didn't even want to make a decision anymore. I willed myself to be content with his decisions. I had adopted an attitude that if I didn't allow myself to want a thing then being denied wouldn't have the power to hurt me. All this effort would not be enough to make this man content enough to stop looking for a reason to demean my efforts, my personality, and my appearance. I walked over to the mirror and identified that I had become absorbed in what I thought he wanted to such an extent that outside of being a Christian I no longer knew who I was or what I wanted.

During this time period of my life, I was listening to a book on tape called Boundaries by Dr. Henry Cloud and Dr. John Townsend. I knew I had to apply the information I was listening to, but I wasn't sure how I was going to do it. This was my first step of courage. Recognizing the truth. Recognizing the need to set a boundary and determining that I would attempt to do so. I knew that I would probably make mistakes but I was willing to take the risk. I had been living quite cautiously from one word to the next or from one activity to the next so as not to ignite my husband's anger. Here I was making a decision that was guaranteed to set him off!

My resolve would soon be tested. One evening as we sat in our living room with our three children surrounding us my husband asked if I was happy. I was not, but I looked around the room and considered the consequence of saying "no." I looked up and said, "Yes, I am." It felt like there was a brick in my stomach.

The next morning as I spent time with the Lord, His Spirit surrounded me and gently impressed upon my thoughts, "Lisa, you know that even when you lie to protect a person's feelings, it's still a lie and I still hate it." This, my friends, is sweet Holy Spirit conviction! I repented by responding, agreeing with God, and asking Him to walk me through change. I cannot emphasize enough what a changing point this was in my life. I was determined to be honest even if the consequences were likely to be painful.

Setting boundaries began with being honest. The next step was saying "no" to demands that were outside of my beliefs, values, and skills. I said "no" to plans for my future employment as a teacher, not because it would be wrong, but because I was sensing that I would not be a good fit in a public school. I knew there was something else, even though I didn't know what. I said "no" to emotional and physical abuse toward our sons. I said "no" to being steered away from supportive relationships. And there were painful consequences. The accusations, restraints, and contempt escalated. My husband's fear of losing control over me resulted in an increased loss of control over himself.

After he physically restrained me and withdrew financial resources, I filed for a legal separation. My divorce felt like one of the biggest failures of my life. It was a broken promise not only to him, but to our children as well. I was completely dependent on the Lord first and then the legal system for survival with my three sons. I also lost friendships due to saying "no." No to adopting rules for my children that other people thought were best. No to sharing personal information. No to others making decisions for me.

But there were blessings as well. A whole new world of freedom opened up to me. I attended church as often as I wanted to. I immersed myself in worship on Sunday afternoons and I started to understand who God created me to be. I learned that I had been avoiding the responsibility of making decisions and dealing with the consequences of them. As I practiced this part of adulthood I became more and more confident in my decision-making ability.

In the pain of wondering how to pay the bills, I decided to go back to school to get a Master's degree. In the process of rediscovering my God-given strengths and talents, I was led to providing therapy through the discipline of social work. As a busy therapist, I never dread going to work. My greatest joy is working "in the Lord." And when the Lord calls me to make a move or enter a new venture I have the freedom and the courage to do so. And now eighteen years later I am experiencing my newest adventure: marriage to a man who accepts, loves, and encourages the woman I have become.

Lisa Parsons

Author Bio

One of the most essential contributions to the overall health of global society, are leaders who aid others, in their personal fight toward maintaining mental and emotional wellness. Leading the way, as a celebrated help throughout her community; is therapist Lisa Parsons (Nelson).

Lisa Parsons is an international best-selling author, educator, communal advocate, and therapist. Having spent many years in the fields of faith-based education and communal mentoring, Lisa decided to shift her love for servant leadership and mental health advocacy into a career that would define her as a critical contributor in the improvement of wellness for all. Having already established a relationship with higher learning, Lisa returned to school in 2008 earning her master's degree with honors in Social Work; an accompaniment to her previous degree in Elementary Education received in 1989. Her passion for mental wellness education, and providing quintessential resources to those in need came easily.

Her mantra is simple; I am empowered to help others move forward to their God-given purpose.

Today Lisa is a reputed therapist and counselor, gifted with an innate ability to change lives. Her wide array of clients all attest to her genius in creating practical approaches to mental wellness. Many have stated that through her practice, Lisa has helped them to drastically improve how they see themselves. Lisa enjoys life as a therapist. It is her hope to expand her advocacy into a broader sphere of influence by implementing technological mediums through blogging and online hosted sessions.

Fear in the Uncertainty of Career Change

~ Amanda Whichard

I had fun in my 20s. After graduating from university, I headed straight to San Francisco to work in advertising. Working as an account executive was everything one could imagine. Late nights, taking clients out to expensive dinners, and free alcohol at the office were just a few of the norms working in the industry. The line between personal and work time was often blurred because, in reality, it all ran together.

Then I turned 30. It's funny how a simple number can make one reevaluate their direction in life. I began to reflect and question my choices. Advertising... Is this really what I want to be doing when I'm 65 years old? One brisk San Francisco night, I was sitting on the balcony with my roommate drinking red wine and talking about life. "I wanted to be a psychologist," I told my roommate. "In high school, I had a vision of becoming a psychologist so I could help people." However, school was difficult for me. I had a hard time concentrating in class. My mind always seemed to wander, no matter how much I tried to focus. I would study for tests and as soon as the test was put in front of me, my mind would go blank like the information was never there. I was also juggling a part-time job and obligations from my business fraternity. Most students were doing the same sorts of things as me, so why was it so hard for me? I would wonder.

One fall morning at university, my psychology advisor scheduled a meeting with me. I'll never forget his knee-high white tube socks and Birkenstock sandals that he wore like part of a uniform. He had that straight shooter New York attitude and I admired him for his intellect and passion when teaching psychology. I looked forward to meeting with him to review the Spring term schedule. Unfortunately, the meeting went in a different direction. Instead of reviewing my schedule, my advisor stated my grades were not good enough to make a career in psychology. "You should think about what else you might want to do," he told me. From his lips to my ears, the words seemed to morph into something that struck deep in my soul. "You aren't *smart* enough," is what I heard. "You aren't *good* enough," is what I told myself. Notice that is not what he said. He said my grades were not good enough. And he was right.

After that crushing yet realistic conversation with my advisor, I decided to change my major. I was glad to find Marketing and Advertising, a field that was glamorous and fast-paced. I enjoyed my career choice for many years, but as time went on those "what if" thoughts continued to creep up in the back of my mind. *What if I would have taken the conversation with my advisor as a challenge? What if I would have retaken classes to improve my grades? Where would I be now?*

"Why don't you go back to school?" my roommate asked on our patio that cool evening. Such a simple question; however, going back to school was something I never wanted to do. I quickly came up with a myriad of reasons why I couldn't: "My graduating GPA isn't good enough"; "It's too expensive"; "I don't have the time"; "I don't want to start over in a new career"; "Maybe when I'm married and have two incomes." There were more than enough excuses, and it felt like there was a mountain between me and my dream career that was just too big to conquer.

As the years passed, I gradually became more and more dissatisfied with my career. I now realize that I had experienced Occupational Burnout. I lost the enthusiasm I once had. I was tired all the time and struggled to get out of bed. My interests and values had evolved and no longer aligned with what I was doing. I felt unfulfilled. That led me to feel anxious and depressed off and on for years.

The year 2016 held a lot of grief for me, and I was at a crossroads at my job. In September of that year, my uncle passed from pancreatic cancer. His passing led to events and connections that would lead to a new path for me.

My phone rang right after I walked into my house following the long drive home from my uncle's funeral. "Hi honey, it's Mom[1] . I met a woman at the funeral that works at a university near us and guess what – they have a graduate psychology program!" I could feel my endorphins spike with excitement and hope. Then just as quickly as the feeling of hope came, those familiar self-doubts began resurfacing. As my mind replayed why it could never happen, I remembered I graduated from college almost 20 years ago! And with that one thought, new worries flooded my mind. Do I even remember how to study? Would I be the oldest student in the class? I failed the first time, why would this time be any different?

Anxiety had once again taken hold of my thoughts, so I took my fears to the only One I knew could help me: my Heavenly Father. "Lord, there are so many changes right now, and so many things point to this being a possibility. But I do not know how to make this work. If this is Your will, I need Your help." And with that prayer, something was different. There was a shift in my mindset and a new determination. I had a longing – a vision for a career helping people through counseling, and signs were pointing that this was the time.

The next day, my phone rang again. "Hi, it's Mom. I called the woman from the university and she gave me the contact information to the dean of the counseling program. Why don't you reach out to her?" Usually, I would have been annoyed with my mother, I am an adult after all, but this time I saw it as an opportunity. I had a longing and a vision for a career helping people through counseling. Now, I had a contact. I put aside my fears and drove across state lines to visit the university campus and meet with the counseling department's dean and advisor. My heart was filled with joy and optimism after that meeting. The career that seemed like a distant dream was starting to come into view. Maybe this could really happen?

As I started taking the steps towards applying for the program, my anxiety and self-doubt tried to hold me back. To manage my anxiety, I chose to focus on one step of the process at a time. That was all I could handle, and I told myself that it was ok. And it was! Each completed step led me closer to becoming a graduate student – something I did not believe I was smart enough, young enough, or financially secure enough for. But God met every need along the way in His perfect timing. Not only was I accepted into graduate school, but I also loved it and excelled at it!

God has been with me every step of the way. When I couldn't see a way to make this career happen, He did. Because when He has a will, He will make a way. What felt like giant rigid mountains in front of me now seem like small ant hills in the rear-view mirror. Making a career change sounded impossible and scary, but what was more frightening was the thought of not attempting it. I concluded that having a few years of starting over would ultimately lead to more fulfillment. My journey is far from over, but I am proud of how far I have come and excited for where God continues to lead me.

Amanda Whichard

Author bio

Amanda Whicard grew up in the greater Houston, Texas area before moving to San Francisco, California in 2001. She focused her early career in digital marketing working at top Advertising agencies with Fortune 500 clients.

In 2016, Amanda began the journey towards a lifelong dream of helping people through psychotherapy. She moved to South Mississippi to begin graduate studies in Counseling Education. Amanda graduated with a 4.0 GPA and achieved the Outstanding Counseling Student Award. Amanda is active in her church and serves as a member of the photography team. She has one fur baby named Honey Bear who has been her companion moving from California to Tennessee to Mississippi. Amanda and Honey Bear enjoy the beach, hiking, and traveling.

Nothing is
Too Broken for God

~ Anne Gillam

My story joyfully began July 31, 2004, in San Angelo, Texas in my parents' backyard. There in the presence of longtime friends, family, and the Justice of Peace, Curtis and I were very happily married. With three children from previous marriages, we believed our love alone would be enough to weather any storm and endure for a lifetime. However, the challenges of a blended family, and relentless life transitions from being active-duty military began to overwhelm, slowly undermine, and tear at the fabric of our marriage.

Far more subversive and damaging for our relationship was the fact that we were two severely broken individuals struggling equally with deep emotional and psychological wounds. I was physically and emotionally abused from my first marriage to the point of torture. For years, I hid the shame of being victimized as if someone would hide a festering wound. After my divorce, I outwardly became a highly independent, career-driven individual, regularly receiving top honors for productivity and drive. However, inwardly, I harbored unforgiveness, deep insecurities, and destructive emotional baggage which regularly manifested itself into my current marriage.

Curtis, on the other hand, was sexually abused as a young child for years. To my surprise and dismay, the stigma of sexual abuse for a young black male living in the south was something no one talked about. Like seeing "Big Foot" in a shopping mall, it was an improbable aberration that simply could not have happened. In fact, when he did bring up the issue of being sexually abused, it was spoken of as a "good thing." Throughout his entire life, he concealed a severe inability to trust, or sustain long-term intimacy with any one of the opposite sex (including myself). As a result, Curtis was often angry and emotionally distant, refusing to confront or even acknowledge the pain of his childhood.

Tragically, within a few years, we were at a severe breaking point and decided to separate with plans for divorce. I found myself a single mom (again), heartbroken and too depressed. Each day I would sit alone in the middle of my bed praying and literally screaming to the top of my lungs for a way out of the pain and sadness. For months, pain and sadness was my travel companion and revealed itself in every aspect of my life, both personal and professional. I could no longer hide.

Fortunately for me (and ultimately for my marriage), my co-worker at the time (turned Pastor) Micah Butterfield took notice and invited me to Northwood Church (NC). For the first time in a long time, I felt unconditional love and acceptance. Still very broken-hearted, every Sunday, for years, I would sit in the same seat at church, pray the same prayer and ask God to change my heart, change Curtis' heart, and fix my marriage. Over and over again... *change my heart, change Curtis' heart, and fix my marriage.* Unwittingly, through the pain, I've learned what King David knew when he stated in Psalm 51:10, "The sacrifices of God are a broken spirit; a broken and contrite heart, O God, you will not despise."

We were separated for nearly three long years when remarkably we began communicating without false pretense or the same anger and unforgiveness of the past, and I (with new hope) invited my estranged husband to NC. In August of 2015, Curtis asked Jesus to come into his heart and change him. Today, part of his testimony is that no one could have changed his heart except for Christ, and I believe it. God miraculously healed our marriage and changed our hearts, turning my sadness into gladness. Equally important, is that by the power of God's spirit Curtis and I have been able to confront and find practical help and restoration from the destructive pain of sexual, emotional, and physical abuse.

Through His mercy for us, we were able to forgive each other and heal long-lasting wounds. On September 2, 2015, we, along with our son, were baptized proclaiming His grace and goodness in our lives. If you are in a difficult situation, press into God and don't lose hope. Curtis and I truly believe that nothing is too broken God can't fix. Christ, through the ministry of Northwood Church, has given us tools and a firm foundation to stand when the storms of life come. Simply cry out to God, He is faithful and just to forgive and restore. Jesus is the answer!

Anne Gillam

Author bio

More than ever, people are looking for solutions; provided by innovative professionals gifted in formulating methods that secure financial futures. Lending a helping hand during these uncertain times; is a rather energetic professional, Anne Gillam.

Anne Gillam is an International Best-Selling Author, consultant, and a Commercial Lines Executive Producer at Anne Gillam is an International Best-Selling Author, consultant, and a Commercial Lines Executive Producer at Southgroup Insurance Gulf Coast. Dominating the insurance business for over 15 years, Anne is reputed for her unmatched ability in building key relationships with businesses along the Mississippi Gulf Coast.

Her mantra is simple; her success is granted only; due to God's grace and mercy upon her life.

As a woman who builds, even her professional vernacular on the principle of serving others as she would serve God; Anne believes that providing exceptional service, conjoined with a genuine love for people; is an uncompromising component of all her accomplishments.

Anne also serves on the Board of Directors for the Women's Resource Center; providing strategic guidance for the center's efforts to assist women facing critical challenges in their lives; while supporting the needs of the unborn child. Anne is also an active team leader in her faith-based community;

championing small group activities, and aiding in pastoral care both for her church and community members.

Anne has built an entire life around serving others.

Appreciated regularly for all she contributes to her local community, Anne was recently recognized by Gulf Coast Woman Magazine, as one of the "100 Successful Women to know" in 2020.

When she is not out changing lives for the better. Anne loves to spend time with her family. She is a wife, daughter, and mother of military veterans, and a proud supporter of military efforts, both locally and around the world.

Anne Gillam, Leader. Philanthropist. Servant.

Broken but Breathing

~ Latasha Bryant

"You are so strong," people often say! My response is, "Not me; God is though!" What they do not know is that I am a brittle, brokenhearted woman trying to find strength to make it daily. You see, our world was turned upside down the night of March 24, 2015, when we received that phone call that our oldest son was just killed. We rushed to the scene, praying it was a mistaken identity only to find that it was true! My worst nightmare, we were living it! His whole life flashed before me, the nineteen years of memories and a lifetime of stolen memories.

Keon was our first child. He was the person that changed my entire world. He gave us the titles of father and mother. I experienced love in a completely new dimension. This little boy helped me to grow to be the woman I am this very day. My thoughts, goals, actions, everything changed when he entered this world. How could he be robbed of a lifetime of nothing but greatness! Sitting at the scene, the scripture entered into my mind, "The Lord giveth and the Lord taketh away" but it was my mother-in-law/Pastor that finished it, "Blessed be the Lord!" That part I was not quite ready to deal with. I mean, how could the Lord, the God that I have faithfully served for over 15 years, allow something like this to happen to my son. I was disappointed with God not protecting him. See, it was another person involved in this incident that suffered life-threatening injuries, but he was still breathing. My thoughts were that was supposed to be Keon; he was not the one that should have succumbed to his injuries. He should have been that testimony! See, I had him active in the church his entire life. He even went on his own as he began to approach adulthood.

So days went by, weeks, months and all I had were memories. We were referred to counseling, which was good to a point, but there was no one that knew what we were feeling, what we were truly dealing with. My husband, Lester; son, Kyrese; and I only had memories. We were determined to make Keon's life count for something. That his name would continue to live on as long as we had breath in our bodies. We established a foundation, "Under His Wings-KRB Foundation." Our goal was to form a group of people who were experiencing the same trauma as we were, bring in some professional and spiritual help, and form a support group for each other. Each year we come together and celebrate the lives of our loved ones, but throughout the year, we provide support to one another as we go through our daily lives.

This foundation began to bring my hope back. Talking and sharing with mothers that were going through the same thing was refreshing. I used the word "refreshing" because grief has a way to make you think you are really going crazy. You see, I could not go crazy, I could not give up! Even though I lost Keon, I still had Kyrese and I had to be that same mother to him. So I began turning my prayers to "Lord, just strengthen me that I will be able to do him as I have done for Keon and strengthen our union, Lester, Kyrese and I that we will be stronger together."

See, my hope had been robbed, my joy was stolen, my peace interrupted, my focus distracted. The devil had me believing that the life I was living was in vain; everything I believed in was not all that it was cracked up to be! In my thoughts, I was thinking that getting saved, living a life according to the word of God, and bringing my children up in the admonishment of the Lord would somehow protect us from any evil doing. That we would be shielded and protected from all hurt, harm, or danger! That we were exempt from the trauma that this life somehow offers you. But all of those were just falsehoods! You see, Jesus Himself went through much trauma when He walked this earth. And if He experienced something like this, why in the world would I be exempt? You see, those fifteen plus years really were an investment for my life and for my children's lives, preparing us for such a time as this!

Keon's life has once again changed my life; my outlook, my goals, and my actions were all reevaluated. We had prepared Keon for his final day not knowing it would come so soon. We learned who and what was important in life: stop sweating the small stuff, enjoy each day as if it were your last, and appreciate God just for who He is and the fact that He sent His Son so that we too can enjoy eternal life. So don't make all these future plans for your children; enjoy your children each day as if you were never going to see them again. Trust God's process and plan for your life even if it doesn't align with yours, and whatever you do share Jesus with your kids; tell them how important it is to have a relationship with Him; teach them to repent and pray. I promise it would be the best INVESTMENT in your life! So when this life throws you things that may break you just breathe and Trust GOD!

Latasha Bryant

Author Bio

Latasha Bryant is a licensed Evangelist, community leader, and a federal government employee for over 12 years. She is the very proud mother of two sons – Keon and Kyrese and has been married to her childhood sweetheart, Lester, for more than 20 years.

After the devastating loss of their oldest son, Keon in 2015, she and her husband formed the Under His Wings - KRB Foundation. The non-profit foundation provides support and resources to families of other homicide victims. Since then, she has continued to work tirelessly as an advocate for crime victims' rights. She regularly coordinates outreach activities with law enforcement and other civic leaders to work to reduce violent crimes along the Mississippi Gulf Coast. She is committed to keeping Keon's legacy alive through her service to the community.

Latasha knows that her faith in God has sustained her during these trying times and hopes and prays that her story will encourage and uplift others.

Overcoming Self-Hatred and Codependency

~ **Racquel Rochelle**

Staring out at the vast open sea, listening to the sound of waves muzzle the faint sounds of an animated movie playing on my phone, I felt frozen. Paralyzed in feelings of shame and disbelief, I kept wondering to myself, "*How did I get here?*" Envying the strength of the waves with its seemingly endless possibilities, I lived in a contrasted reality. At the moment, I was a single mother, homeless, heartbroken, and unrecognizable to myself with hardly anything to my name. With an innocent toddler face staring at me in excitement over our "beach movie night" I became an imposter and pretended to be strong. But internally, I wanted to cry my soul out and scream nonstop. I was deeply wounded in my soul and wanted nothing more than to let my true feelings out. But instead, as a single mother without a break, I suppressed as usual and continued to wonder just how did I, a young intelligent Racquel filled with so much promise, get here.

The Set Up:

Growing up as a deeply dark-skinned intelligent girl in Mississippi, I attracted a lot of negative attention. I was teased and bullied due to my intelligence and complexion for as long as I could remember. *Burnt cookie*.... *Oreo*.... *Oil*.... *Black Skillet*...were a few nicknames imposed upon me. I had no consistent friends and was known as the black sheep of my family. Rejection quickly became a normal part of my existence. Seeming as though I only received attention in the form of verbal abuse, physical abuse, years of molestation, and constant bullying for just being myself, I quickly despised attention and tried to avoid it at all cost. So I became a quiet child with her head down in books. I suppressed my voice, talents, and intellect and worked hard to blend into the background. My mother and sisters were extensively known in the community. But me, I was just Jackie's daughter...the little sister of the popular girls... a Gardner girl with no known identity of her own. The one without a name. Just a little black girl who is smart but is quiet. The black sheep. As a teenager, my family moved to a predominantly white city and so my invisibility grew even thicker. This was until I was old enough to work. It was then that I began to receive a different kind of attention. Some coworkers and customers seemed to take a liking to my appearance. I was smart enough to realize that it was lust but honestly at the moment, I didn't care. It was "positive" attention so I accepted it. It was nice. I had a nice shape and it often had me falsely accused of being sexually active but I didn't mind. I finally had an attribute that attracted something other than the abuse and bullying that I was accustomed to. At least I thought.... but this body I held so dearly attracted me right into a cycle of toxic relationships, the worse beginning in 2010.

The Cycle

He was my best friend and fatal attraction all wrapped in one. I met him online and the high I felt from his attention was insurmountable. I felt so seen and adored by him. Knowing all the right things to say, he satisfied a void created by years of being torn down and quenched a longstanding thirst I had for connection, love, and positive attention. But at some point, things shifted. He transitioned from being an external source of compliments to becoming my point of reference for my identity. He had a way of making me feel so alive in the highs of our relationship but could equally murder any ounce of esteem and worth I had whenever times would get bad. The same lips that expressed his love for me also expressed how I would never be treated the way I thought I should be treated. He made sure that I knew that I wasn't a princess and this wasn't a movie. The passion grew stronger but the fights became louder and more aggressive until physical abuse settled itself into the norm of our relationship. I had a way of downplaying the severity of abuse I encountered. I filled my head with *"Oh he was drunk..." "Well I did make him upset...*" *"He isn't always this way..."* and countless other excuses to pacify the pain and get us back to our "happy place." He cheated on me regularly and lived on my income but he was mine. This toxic romance was my comfort. It connected to the familiarity of the mistreatment from my youth but it added a layer of attention I craved. It was my truth. He shattered that truth the moment he hit me in front of my 1-month-old baby. I didn't want her to grow up accustomed to this. The love I had for her that I somehow lost for myself empowered me to attempt to break the cycle. But it wasn't easy.

The Shift

Once leaving him, I found myself making rash decisions. I felt so crushed and like I just could not function without a man. Trying to get over him, I busied myself with countless 16 hr shifts and meaningless connections with men. I abruptly gave up the home we rented together with no plans of a new place because it reminded me of him. I inevitably made myself homeless. Hopping from couch to couch, I spent little to no time on facing myself, renewing my mind, and getting to know who I was authentically. My identity was in a man who was no longer around. I ran from every opportunity of getting to know myself because I simply didn't like me. Why would I like me? The core of me seemed to attract every form of heartache and abandonment imaginable. I seemed to never fit in. I wasn't a valuable part of anyone's life. I figured I only mattered to my daughter because she was forced to be mine. I felt that I could die and it would take so many days for anyone to notice. But even as soothing as suicide sounded at the moment, I also had to fail at that because of my child. Imagine that. I couldn't even succeed at suicide. My love for her saved me yet again. Managing to self-sabotage every opportunity presented to me beyond college due to not believing in myself, I had very little to show for myself. Outside of making money and entertaining men, what did I have to offer the world? So why like me? I couldn't so I didn't try. This numb, detached, and toxic cycle was my reality for a long time and I found comfort in it. But all of that was shattered by the death of my grandmother.

The Surrender

Hopelessly watching her fight for and lose her last breath, I had never felt so useless than in that moment. And here it was the woman who believed in me the most. In her eyes I was a doctor, Sojourner Truth, Maya Angelou, and Rosa Parks rolled into one and she had great expectations for my life. How could I let her die without seeing a glimpse of her expectations coming to past? How could I fail her like that? These questions and her last moments haunted me for weeks. It was a desperation and hopelessness that I couldn't put into words. Sitting there on the beach shore, I came to a point where I just couldn't go on with an empty, broken, toxic, destructive, codependent existence anymore. No amount of wishful thinking could bring back all of my losses but I could decide to stop losing. I didn't know what to do but I knew of at least one who did know... God. I grew up with an awareness of him but I needed more than an awareness in this moment. I needed truth, guidance, and tangible experiences. I needed a relationship. God worked on me in stages to free my mindset from this toxic way of thinking. Those stages involved stripping, realigning, and connecting. First, I was stripped of everything I could attach my identity to and in the moment it felt awful. I felt unstable in every sense. But in that year God showed me how much of a responsibility he takes on in providing for me. I was forced to see myself naked and see the potential hidden within the uniqueness of me. Realizing that my relationships with men were counterproductive to cultivating self-love, I left the guy I was dating before discovering I was pregnant. During this time alone, God helped me to realign the way I saw myself. Ghosted through the pregnancy, I stumbled upon the Women's Resource Center and discovered a passion for helping other women with a past like mine. I was laid off due to pregnancy complications but finding a job as a substitute teacher catapulted me into a career as a certified teacher and gave me an opportunity to mentor teenage girls. I was struggling to keep my new apartment but the housing assistance I had forgotten I applied for 3 years earlier had finally been approved. My car was repossessed twice but somehow I was able to pay it off by the year's end. Learning to see and accept the love of God, he also brought me into the stage of authentically connecting with others. I now have like-minded friends with whom I'm able to be vulnerable and transparent as we learn to give and receive love from each other. Today's reality is so drastically different than my darkest hour and I can't contribute it to anything other than the practical and tangible work of God in my life. Becoming an educator, mentor, author, homeowner, entrepreneur, and influencer is more than what I could ever see myself becoming. Since he has done it for me, I am more than willing to be a mouthpiece and let others know that he can certainly do it for them.

Staring out at the vast open sea, listening to the sound of waves muzzle the faint sounds of an animated movie playing on my phone, I felt frozen. Paralyzed in feelings of shame and disbelief, I kept wondering to myself, *"How did I get here?"* Envying the strength of the waves with its seemingly endless possibilities, I lived in a contrasted reality. At the moment, I was a single mother, homeless, heartbroken, and unrecognizable to myself with hardly anything to my name. With an innocent toddler face staring at me in excitement over our "beach movie night" I became an imposter and pretended to be strong. But internally, I wanted to cry my soul out and scream nonstop. I was deeply wounded in my soul and wanted nothing more than to let my true feelings out. But instead, as a single mother without a break, I suppressed as usual and continued to wonder just how did I, a young intelligent Racquel filled with so much promise, get her...

The Set Up:
Growing up as a deeply dark-skinned intelligent girl in Mississippi, I attracted a lot of negative attention. I was teased and bullied due to my intelligence and complexion for as long as I could remember. *Burnt cookie.... Oreo.... Oil.... Black Skillet...*were a few

nicknames imposed upon me. I had no consistent friends and was known as the black sheep of my family. Rejection quickly became a normal part of my existence. Seeming as though I only received attention in the form of verbal abuse, physical abuse, years of molestation, and constant bullying for just being myself, I quickly despised attention and tried to avoid it at all cost. So, I became a quiet child with her head down in books. I suppressed my voice, talents, and intellect and worked hard to blend into the background. My mother and sisters were extensively known in the community. But me, I was just Jackie's daughter...the little sister of the popular girls... a Gardner girl with no known identity of her own. The one without a name. Just a little black girl who is smart but is quiet. The black sheep. As a teenager, my family moved to a predominantly white city and so my invisibility grew even thicker. This was until I was old enough to work. It was then that I began to receive a different kind of attention. Some coworkers and customers seemed to take a liking to my appearance. I was smart enough to realize that it was lust but honestly at the moment, I didn't care. It was "positive" attention so I accepted it. It was nice. I had a nice shape and it often had me falsely accused of being sexually active but I didn't mind. I finally had an attribute that attracted something other than the abuse and bullying that I was accustomed to. At least I thought....but this body I held so dearly attracted me right into a cycle of toxic relationships, the worse beginning in 2010.

The Cycle

He was my best friend and fatal attraction all wrapped in one. I met him online and the high I felt from his attention was insurmountable. I felt so seen and adored by him. Knowing all the right things to say, he satisfied a void created by years of being torn down and quenched a longstanding thirst I had for connection, love, and positive attention. But at some point, things shifted. He transitioned from being an external source of compliments to becoming my point of reference for my identity. He had a way of making me feel so alive in the highs of our relationship but could equally murder any ounce of esteem and worth I had whenever times would get bad. The same lips that expressed his love for me also expressed how I would never be treated the way I thought I should be treated. He made sure that I knew that I wasn't a princess and this wasn't a movie. The passion grew stronger but the fights became louder and more aggressive until physical abuse settled itself into the norm of our relationship. I had a way of downplaying the severity of abuse I encountered. I filled my head with *"Oh he was drunk..." "Well I did make him upset..." "He isn't always this way..."* and countless other excuses to pacify the pain and get us back to our "happy place." He cheated on me regularly and lived on my income but he was mine. This toxic romance was my comfort. It connected to the familiarity of the mistreatment from my youth but it added a layer of attention I craved. It was my truth. He shattered that truth the moment he hit me in front of my 1-month-old baby. I didn't want her to grow up accustomed to this. The love I had for her that I somehow lost for myself empowered me to attempt to break the cycle. But it wasn't easy.

The Shift

Once leaving him, I found myself making rash decisions. I felt so crushed and like I just could not function without a man. Trying to get over him, I busied myself with countless 16 hr shifts and meaningless connections with men. I abruptly gave up the home we rented together with no plans of a new place because it reminded me of him. I inevitably made myself homeless. Hopping from couch to couch, I spent little to no time on facing myself, renewing my mind, and getting to know who I was authentically. My identity was in a man who was no longer around. I ran from every opportunity of getting to know myself because I simply didn't like me. Why would I like me? The core of me seemed to attract every form of heartache and abandonment imaginable. I seemed to never fit in. I wasn't a valuable part of anyone's life. I figured I only mattered to my daughter because she was forced to be mine. I felt that I could die and it would take so many days for anyone to notice. But even as soothing as suicide sounded at the moment, I also had to fail at that because of my child. Imagine that. I couldn't even succeed at suicide. My love for her saved me yet again. Managing to self-sabotage every opportunity presented to me beyond college due to not believing in myself, I had very little to show for myself. Outside of making money and entertaining men, what did I have to offer the world? So why like me? I couldn't so I didn't try. This numb, detached, and toxic cycle was my reality for a long time and I found comfort in it. But all of that was shattered by the death of my grandmother.

The Surrender

Hopelessly watching her fight for and lose her last breath, I had never felt so useless than in that moment. And here it was the woman who believed in me the most. In her eyes I was a doctor, Sojourner Truth, Maya Angelou, and Rosa Parks rolled into one and she had great expectations for my life. How could I let her die without seeing a glimpse of her expectations coming to past? How could I fail her like that? These questions and her last moments haunted me for weeks. It was a desperation and hopelessness that I couldn't put into words. Sitting there on the beach shore, I came to a point where I just couldn't go on with an empty, broken, toxic, destructive, codependent existence anymore. No amount of wishful thinking could bring back all of my losses but I could decide to stop losing. I didn't know what to do but I knew of at least one who did know... God. I grew up with an awareness of him but I needed more than an awareness in this moment. I needed truth, guidance, and tangible experiences. I needed a relationship. God worked on me in stages to free my mindset from this toxic way of thinking. Those stages involved stripping, realigning, and connecting. First, I was stripped of everything I could attach my identity to and in the moment it felt awful. I felt unstable in every sense. But in that year God showed me how much of a responsibility he takes on in providing for me. I was forced to see myself naked and see the potential hidden within the uniqueness of me. Realizing that my relationships with men were counterproductive to cultivating self-love, I left the guy I was dating before discovering I was pregnant. During this time alone, God helped me to realign the way I saw myself. Ghosted through the pregnancy, I stumbled upon the Women's Resource Center and discovered a passion for helping other women with a past like mine. I was laid off due to pregnancy complications but finding a job as a substitute teacher catapulted me into a career as a certified teacher and gave me an opportunity to mentor teenage girls. I was struggling to keep my new apartment but the housing assistance I had forgotten I applied for 3 years earlier had finally been approved. My car was repossessed twice but somehow, I was able to pay it off by the year's end. Learning to see and accept the love of God, he also brought me into the stage of authentically connecting with others. I now have like-minded friends with whom I'm able to be vulnerable and transparent as we learn to give and receive love from each other. Today's reality is so drastically different than my darkest hour and I can't contribute it to anything other than the practical and tangible work of God in my life. Becoming an educator, mentor, author, homeowner, entrepreneur, and influencer is more than what I could ever see myself becoming. Since he has done it for me, I am more than willing to be a mouthpiece and let others know that he can certainly do it for them.

Racquel Rochelle

Author Bio

Born in Atlanta but raised in South Mississippi, Racquel Rochelle is an educator with a passion for advocating for healthy minds, finances, and relationships. A single mother of two girls, she is devoted to overcoming a blinding abusive past and has set out to break the barriers of codependency and generational toxic mindsets to fulfill her purpose in life while motivating others around her to do the same. Advocating for financial freedom and the dismantling of harmful realities such as colorism, loyalty to toxic relationships, destructive self-perception, and self-sabotage, she works with individuals and small groups to define their ideal selves and provides accountability and support as they journey there. With faith as her center and through her role in education and various forms of artistic expression she promotes that every person has an invaluable existence and someone somewhere is depending upon that person to own and live up to that truth.

Uncommon Forgiveness

~ **Sondra Striker**

"Forgiveness does not mean one forgets the offense, but that in spite of the memory, one erases the debt."
- Voddie Baucham,

"Forgiveness does not mean one forgets the offense, but that in spite of the memory, one erases the debt."
- Voddie Baucham,

The road to forgiveness of my abuser began with a phone call. I called Mom's house, thinking she would answer as she always did, but not this time. My brother answered the phone, and it wasn't long before he started telling me about his latest mishap: Someone had broken his jaw while he was in the wrong place at the wrong time...again. Nothing was ever his fault; someone else always had to take the blame for the decisions he made in life. Including him molesting me for eight years from ages 6-14. As I listened to his excuses - the shame, rage, anger, and frankly hate I felt for him boiled over, and I spat out the words, "You deserve everything you get!!" I slammed the phone down, shaking with all the frustration I'd felt for years after every encounter I had with him.

Within 15 seconds, the phone rang, and I heard the words that sent me into a tailspin, "What did I ever do to you that would make you say something like that to me?" My stomach clenched, and I felt sick; the room closed in on me just like it had so many times before. In an instant, the words were out of my mouth, "Are you kidding me, you really don't know why I'd say something like that to you?" His next words took me out, "You're still not over that, how long are you going to keep bringing that up?" And finally, he told me I was a horrible person for saying that he deserved what he got.

Once again, I hung up...and I spent about 2 hours crying, wailing. Again, my abuser had made me feel shame. It was all my fault that he had abused me all those years ago. It was a never-ending scenario I couldn't seem to make stop. Even with years of therapy and medications, it was still consuming me, eating away at me from somewhere deep inside that would not heal. I was 38 years old, on my 5th husband, and I still let this demon come roaring back at me without a moment's notice. The forgiveness that I knew God would give him just wasn't within me.

I thought I had forgiven him after I accepted Christ. Still, every time I was in the same room with him, the old feelings came rushing back, and I was back to square one - shame, guilt, hate for my inability to let it go. But even though I was a saved Christian, I didn't really have much of a relationship with my Savior. Nor did I know how to forgive in such a way that my heart would heal so that the old feelings would no longer hold me captive.

But God...

A few days after the call, we headed to my husband's family farm for a mini family reunion. The awful words were still rolling around in my head; my emotions were in shreds. I was desperate to have someone tell me that I wasn't a "bad" person, even though my husband had done so a dozen times - I needed God to think I was a "good" person.

The sweetest, most godly woman I had known thus far in my life was my late mother-in-law, Amy. She was the first person in my husband's family to love me. She was confined to a wheelchair. I remember always wanting to be of service to her - brushing her with her hair, picking the right jewelry out, or helping her in the kitchen. She was a gentle, loving, accepting woman who had faith as big as a mountain. So it's no wonder that I sought her out that weekend to help me work through the thoughts of being unworthy not only to God but also to my husband and even my family. I explained what had happened a few days before and asked why I couldn't get over the past.

Why could I not forgive him once and for all? The long and short of it was this, how do I forgive him so that I could be in the same room with him without all the emotion taking me over? And her answer to me was this, "Sondra, even when you forgive someone, that doesn't mean that God expects you to immediately be over it. It takes time." But the next words she spoke are what really helped set me free and begin the long journey to forgiveness, "You don't have to have a relationship with him to forgive him. It's not necessary to be in the same room with him; you can tell your family that you don't want to be around him for a while." It was as simple as that! It was up to me to stand up for myself and tell people what I needed. And it's been that way for 19 years. I haven't had any contact with my abuser, my family has respected my wishes, and I have forgiven my brother.

Yes, it did take time for the forgiveness to feel real and be cemented in my heart. When my mother was ill in 2019, one thing on my mind was that someone needed to tell my brother, who was in prison, that she had cancer and might not live long. I didn't feel the burden to go to him myself, but I knew in my heart that he deserved to hear it as soon as possible; it was the right thing to do. My mom passed away early on a Sunday morning in November; sadly, my nephew couldn't speak to my brother before her death. I think about him sometimes, finding out that his mother died and he didn't even know she was ill, but now my heart doesn't tighten at the thought of him. I don't feel the pain or anger anymore. Instead, I can feel compassion, maybe not love yet, but it feels good not to have a hole in my heart anymore.

And the advice my mother-in-law had given me all those years ago still holds true today. Forgiveness takes time, and sometimes it's done from a distance, but no matter what, Jesus died for all of us to be forgiven and set free. Will God eventually restore the relationship with my brother? Well, that's up to Him. If He tells me it's time, then it's time, and I know He'll prepare the way for it to happen.

Sandra Striker

Author Bio

Sondra was born in upstate New York into a big Italian family. Her mom and dad moved the family, her and her 3 brothers to Texas in 1971 and she grew up in Cleburne. Sondra married Mark Striker in 2000 and they traveled the world during his Air Force career. They lived in England and the Azores, and enjoyed traveling in Europe until Mark retired in 2012 and they settled in Gulfport MS. Since then Sondra has been active in lots of different volunteer roles including her home church Northwood Church and Women's Resource Center, for 7+ years.

Sondra has one son TJ, who is 41, and three dogs all rescues that she calls her tiny little humans-Sadie Mae, Holly Belle, and Tuxedo. Her biggest joys in life are knowing Jesus, being a mom to humans and dogs, and being Mark's wife.

It's Time for a Change

~ **Charlotte McLaurin**

"Uncommon Courage" is not the term I would use for my situation – being able to shoulder the responsibility of a consistently troubled son. I believed this blessing of a son was truly God's gift, and I honestly thought I should do like Hanna did and give him to the church. Well... being as I was in the twentieth century and not in Bible days, the church raising the child took on a whole new meaning. I was a new Christian, just to let you know, so I took God's word literally. The church I attended as a new convert, was interested in other points, like my singleness and a child, so from the onset, I had to cling onto Christ for more reasons than one.

My son was an active blessing from day one; always moving with a mind of his own. He seemed content to ride his Big Wheel from the living room to the bedroom while I sat on the couch and studied. I learned to have conversations with the Lord early on. Mostly asking, "What am I gonna do, Lord? This boy... ugh!" When he was two, I asked one of the mothers of the church if I could just beat him until my arms got tired - then beat him some more. She said, "Daughter, no, there is something else going on here." She never got a chance to clarify what she meant by that. Doctors said to wait until he was in school. School said to take him to the doctors. So... the diagnosis from both was Attention Deficit with Hyperactivity Disorder (ADHD). Heavy on the hyper, but the Lord said he would be a mouthpiece to his generation - Yeah, right!

Can we just say from literally A to Z, my son exhibited behaviors that called for some attention of one sort or another? Seemed like many people, if not all he met, would do okay with him at first, but then a slow withdrawal would begin because his "hyper" was a turnoff. Who gets kicked out of after school daycare at four years old because he can sleep better under his cot? He was not disturbing others, but he could go to sleep better that way. It was a problem because it was not the conventional way to do nap time. I said, "Who cares?? HE'S ASLEEP and not bothering anyone for 45 minutes! Relish the quiet!"

Needless to say, these behaviors continued. I talked so much to God; asking why, praying, crying, literally begging for answers. I was utterly exhausted most of the time, and to add to my situation, I had a second child, later a third child, and then an adopted child. You see, I read somewhere in the Bible that two were better than one, but I should have studied that just a little more. You would look at this handsome, well-mannered little fellow, and you could not tell of the turmoil going on in his head.

Social workers and the school felt therapy and learning various techniques to demonstrate the correct behaviors would work. The doctors said medicate, and at that point, I said, "Let's do this." I could not provide for the family and keep up at the pace my son wanted to move. Warp speed is the term I would use to describe his movements. Pills, sports, and therapy followed through the next years. Sports seemed to be incredibly beneficial and helped control his need for speed. Still, he was lethargic at times on the medication. I tried other natural methods under the doctor's direction because the medicine seemed experimental in its application. The unorthodox behavior in the classroom drove his teachers mad. I was called by the school almost every day! I said, "Can you just overlook it please?" His behavior affected the classroom environment so much that his teachers and classmates began to be ugly in their treatment of my son. My empathy fighting on his behalf would prove detrimental in the long run as I look back on all this. I dreaded each time my phone rang during the day.

It was also very difficult caring for my other children because he constantly demanded my attention in some form or fashion. I was always calling him to get off of the wall, get out of the tree, get off of the train tracks - you name it. At times, I would begin to feel like my heart was sinking into my chest, and dread would come. I had a "fight or flight" response all the time. He told me what my lot was. I figured, "God, You said You would never leave me nor forsake me, and in my questioning in the early years, You told me what his lot was." I guessed all this was part of the process, but thought, "Please hurry and get there before I pass out."

Jail, court systems, missed graduation, rebellion, name-calling, defiance, nice smile, pretty boy, demon-possessed, fine athlete, unteachable, bucking authority, fighting, shot at... all this with a superman mentality. "God, please stop the madness," I thought. How much more before this mouthpiece emerges? All the while I was thinking, "Okay, we got through this one", " By your Grace, Father, we overcame that one", "Lord, I am still standing". No tears were falling, even though I was crying, needing relief from it all.

I could give my son much grace because I knew much of his systematic issues were from years of drug abuse by me with conception happening less than thirty days after I quit using. I panicked the entire nine months carrying him. I did not know what to expect. I read a lot, and all signs pointed towards a child having neurological problems from the parent's drug use. Of course, guilt was glad to take up residence in the midst of the mess with no letup of pity. I asked God if He could see this crushed heart in my hands. "I am offering it to you in exchange for healing and happiness. I've given, I've begged, I've prayed." I did not mention earlier, but I cried so much till I did not think I had any water left in my body. I spent many a night sitting on the tub in my bathroom, trying to hear my next steps from the Lord, because I just could not take another step without His help.

He's 31 now and I look back at my Mercy and Grace. They have been in a battle and are still holding strong. Through all this, I finished two degrees, raised two other children plus my adopted son, and my two granddaughters.

Lord, I'm still here. I'm thinking surely, You're ready to change him. I believed I had to be ready for him when he was converted. Then that would make all this make sense. All this was and is for my growing, and maturing, into the God-woman I need to be for the ministry of Your people, Lord.

Yes, there is more. The day he was found unresponsive in my yard, I said, "Father, I know You didn't have me go through all this all these years just to let him die." Now that would be jacked up. He survived, but I have learned from times past not to exhale too soon! Yep, Yep, Yep! He did rehabilitation for about four months and the prognosis appeared to be good. I tried not to be weakened, and even though I say there was progress, but not lasting improvement. Those months on my own were peaceful considering for thirty years before that there could have been an outbreak of crazy at any turn. Since I had not known that kind of peace before in my surroundings, I exhaled and went on vacation.

Through other events unknown to me, my son was not strong enough nor grounded enough in Christ to stand toe-to-toe with the enemy of his soul. His superman mentality lured him into thinking he could handle it. He's not exactly right back into the same mess, but I'm not the same Mama either. This is where I think this Uncommon Courage comes into play.

Who has undergirded and helped me to pick up and keep going? *"Ooo, Ooo, I know, I know!"* God and His Grace.

Where have I found strength and encouragement on a regular basis? God's word.

What have I been doing instead of pulling my now very gray hair out? Standing on the truths in God's word.

How, how, how, have I made it this far without literally wanting to sit down anywhere and just cry and whine "whoa is me" and feel sorry for myself? God's Mercy and Grace brought me through.

I must daily follow the example of unconditional love Jesus displayed. No, I do not succeed every day. I play this moment-by-moment. There are days when it seems worse than before. My son is still trying as best as he's able and I'm still standing, firmly grounded in the promise of His salvation and the full conversion of my son into the mouthpiece to his generation.

I can only give thanks for the change. I give thanks in advance for his change.

Charlotte McLaurin

Author Bio

A transplant from the beautiful State of Maryland, I have resided in Gulfport, MS for the last 20 Years. I earned my Bachelors of Arts Degree in Business Administration and I'm currently studying for my MBA. I've also earned the Society of Human Resource's Management Certified Professional Accreditation. I bring over 25 years of experience serving up Customer Service VIP. I served 10 years in the United States Army as a Personnel Manager and spent 5 years in Banking and Mortgage Lending.

The last 13 years were spent with the Gulfport Job Corps Center as the Human Resources Specialist. I am currently an Avon Representative and studying to become a Virtual Assistant. I work diligently winning souls and making disciples with my family Northwood Church, where I mentor young women and serve as a Warrior with the Prayer team ministries. My latest venture is as a Co-Author of Leading with Uncommon Courage and lastly, reestablishing my business, Services Development on the Rise, a Business Services Corporation.

Breaking Through the Boundaries

~ MeLisa Dill

I was chatting with a good friend of mine the other day on the phone. She made this statement to me, 'You know MeLisa, you are really livin' the dream.' To be honest, it kind of shocked me. It's something that I've felt a deep appreciation for and something that I have recognized for my own reality but not really something that I considered others would take notice of. We've been close for over 10 years and she's my friend with whom I have all those crazy late-night conversations. You know the ones where you solve all the world's problems and then complain that you can't get the kids to put the clothes actually in the clothes basket instead of beside it? Yes, she is that friend for me. So, of course, she has seen my journey up close and personal but... But her using those words to describe my life was so humbling.

You see growing up, I had always struggled with fitting in. Coming from a poor family, I didn't have the nice things or clothes that other kids had. I wasn't the pretty one or had an infectious personality. I was the quiet, untamed curly-haired girl that was completely socially awkward - and if I'm being honest, still very much am. My self-confidence was low but I always had a burning desire to succeed. I wanted people to see me for me, I wanted to prove to them that I had value. Isn't that what we all want, just to be seen, liked, and appreciated?

So if this tells you anything, I was the first in my family to actually graduate from high school. There was no real expectation beyond that. My grades couldn't get me to college and there were no goals or direction set for what was next. What was I going to do with my life?

A year out of high school, I joined the US Navy and served our great country for six years. It was at that point that I met and married my wonderful husband. He introduced me to Jesus Christ and I learned what an amazing Savior we have. It was in Him and through Him, I could do great things! My husband and I eventually had four adventurous boys whom I was fortunate to stay home with.

Life was so good but after being an at-home-mom for about ten years, I wanted something just for me. I still had something I wanted to give the world - like there was still more. With little education and not much work experience, what was I going to do though? Couple those facts with the story I had told myself for years that I didn't have value, I basically put up boundaries for myself that haunted me like a professionally built Halloween house.

I was excited to find a job though, it was flexible and it was as if all of my life skills were finally coming together and making sense. I started in customer service and then worked my way up to operations manager of a local 7 figure mom and pop shop. I LOVED my job! I learned so much about myself in that position. I figured out things like websites, marketing, operations, and a whole host of other skills that I never thought I would be able to understand. But it all came with a price. I was working all the time and stressed. My marriage was suffering, I was neglecting so many of my kid's needs and feeling guilty, and to be honest, the work environment was toxic. It wasn't worth it, but what instead?

On top of the aforementioned issues, we decided to sell our house and build. It felt like I was in a game of sticks. For those of you who don't remember this, ehem 'older' game, it's where you toss a stack of sticks on the table and try to remove one stick at a time without disturbing another. I was afraid the whole stack was going to crumble at any point. It finally did when my boss came to me and said that she needed more hours from me. And if I didn't give them to her then she would be forced to hire someone new and I would end up training them out of my job. She knew I needed the job for the build and this was what she thought would be motivation for me to give her more. The only thing I saw at that point was no one was going to look out for my family but me. My marriage,

My kids, My life was going to be My responsibility and I was never going to allow anyone to shake that foundation again.

I prayed SO hard at that point! I finally valued myself and my abilities and I started scouring the internet to try to figure out how to work from home and actually make legitimate money. That is when the Lord showed me Virtual Assistance (VA) work. I can be hard-headed at times and He had to put this in front of me several times. Just me? VAs are essentially independent contractors providing admin type skills to a business virtually. So with more prayer, I felt like God answered. With that still small voice, He told me that I could quit my job and everything would be ok. He never promised riches or fame, but it would be ok. Never in a million years could I have imagined how amazing 'ok' was going to be!

In the middle of building a house, right before Christmas time, I stepped out in faith and trusted God's word to quit my job and start a business at nearly 40yrs old. I used a course from an online company called The Virtual Savvy. It was amazing because God placed me on the founder's, Abbey Ashely, heart, and she decided to gift me the course for Christmas. It was 2016 when I started a VA business and actually made legitimate money from home - on My time, under My terms. Seeing more potential, I continued my education in the online space and earned my Online Business Manager (OBM) Certification and later also earned my Director of Operations Certification. But before I even received the first certification, I landed a big client! Abbey herself reached out to me to contract for my OBM services in 2017. That relationship grew and in 2018 I became the Chief of Operations of The Virtual Savvy. We help individuals start, grow, and scale their own Virtual Assistant business from scratch. Together, Abbey and I have grown this business into a multi-million dollar company! It is a wonderful, full-circle story and I am helping other people find the same freedom that I did! I work from my new beautiful home, make amazing money, take lavish business trips, and most importantly, I am present for my family. My marriage is strong and I have been able to be an advocate for my kids through different challenges. This is truly livin' the dream!

I hope that you caught all of what happened here. None of it was me, it was *all* the Lord orchestrating this journey. All I did was be obedient to His direction and lean into the courage he put in my heart. When I finally trusted in Him it all started to change and boundaries that I once put on myself were broken down. I am grateful and humbled every day that God gives me.

Here is what I hope you take away:

1. I'll just let the scripture speak for itself for the first one. Trust in the LORD with all thine heart; and lean not unto thine own understanding. *In all thy ways acknowledge him, and he shall direct thy paths. ~Proverbs 3:5-6*

2. It doesn't matter what your education/ background is. God has put greatness in each of us. YOU are in control of your life - you through Christ! The online space is full of opportunities to learn and grow, utilize all resources! *For I know the plans I have for you, declares the LORD, plans to prosper you and not to harm you, plans to give you hope and a future. ~Jeremiah 29:11*

3. I started a brand new journey 'later in life' in the online space. There is an opportunity for anyone out there with the drive to make it happen! *I can do all things through Christ which strengtheneth me. ~Phillippians 4:13*

4. Don't let the devil win the head game. So many times I let my own self-doubt and other's opinions of me define me & it was all lies. *For God hath not given us the spirit of fear; but of power, and of love, and of a sound mind. ~2 Timothy 1:7*

Praying my story helps to inspire you to find Uncommon Courage to break through those boundaries that hinder you!

Melisa Dill

Author Bio

Today's innovators are viewed as essential gears propelling the world forward.

Whether breakthrough is taking place in strategic operations, team building, or business finance, the global community moves swiftly, at the mercy of its innovators. Creating seamless rhythm and undeniable traction in all three; is business guru, MeLisa Dill.

MeLisa Dill is an International Best-Selling Author, Certified Online Business Manager, Certified Director of Operations, and the Chief Operating Officer of a multi-seven figure company, The Virtual Savvy.

Driven by a reluctance to settle for a life, controlled by corporate arenas, MeLisa joined The Virtual Savvy; a brand focused on the organization of creating efficient backend systems while keeping the heart of clientele in mind. The Virtual Savvy, offers innovative platforms for entrepreneurs and business professionals; to start, grow, and scale their own Virtual Assistance businesses. Since 2016, MeLisa Dill has established a plethora of clients and played a heavy hand in helping individuals find success and freedom through online work, and MeLisa Dill to be one of the most sought-after strategists in online business.

Her mantra is simple: Her steps are led by a divine faith in God and a heart for people.

Since joining the establishment of The Virtual Savvy, MeLisa has been an inspiration for many women longing for professional change. With a sincere love, to help them break free from corporate structures and the grind of having someone else determine their future, MeLisa takes professionals; from having a desire to do something different to providing them with a myriad of options guaranteed to end in their ultimate success.

As a trusted member in the business society, MeLisa Dill remains a remarkable innovator on various entrepreneurial forefronts.

When she is not busy helping professionals execute their next million-dollar strategy, she is a valued member of her local community and loved dearly by family and friends.

MeLisa Dill. Leader. Innovator. Energizer.

It is Only a Mirage

~ Rachel Robinson

*"But when I am afraid, I will put my
trust in you."*
Psalms 56:3 NLT

*"But when I am afraid, I will put my
trust in you."*
Psalms 56:3 NLT

This was the first scripture that I taught my then 3-year-old daughter. I wanted her to know that there will be times when she will be afraid. There will be times when fear will rise and try to make her question her identity. There will be times when she will face hurdles of fear and adversity on the road to accomplishing her dreams and goals. I wanted her to know these things in her early years because I, as an adult, was learning them too. I wanted her to know that it is okay to be afraid, but not to stay afraid. I was becoming more aware of how my childhood trauma would affect her if I did not learn to overcome the very thing I was teaching her. You might be wondering why I began this chapter referencing my daughter and my title says, "It is Only a Mirage." Well, let me explain.

When I was a young, adolescent girl, my mother, my sister, and I lived in fear. I did not know that's what it was called at the time, but in hindsight, fear resounds throughout my childhood. It was normal for me. My mother, may she continue to rest in peace, was a strong woman who had faced many trials and had a tumultuous set of circumstances in her life, those of which left her somewhat jaded, resentful, and afraid. She was afraid to love to her fullest capacity. My mother was afraid of letting others love and see her. She was afraid to allow her faith to guide her pursuit of certain goals. Fear was allowed to rob her of many of God's tangible promises. Ultimately, the fear created such a deficit in our lives that poverty seemed endless. It enlisted me into a vicious cycle until I decided to be free from it.

See, fear creates a bondage that's more adhesive than gorilla glue. It will entangle you and cause you to think that there are limits to what you can achieve. It will set up strongholds in your mind and cause you to believe that certain promises, gifts, abundance, prosperity, love, wealth, etc. are intangible. You will begin to rehearse these lies. Unfortunately, this is why many people never overcome and break through the harsh environment. Fear continuously holds a dress rehearsal dinner and serves food that looks deliciously appetizing but tastes like last Wednesday's trash. Even so, I'm writing this to tell you that it is only a mirage. What is a mirage, you ask? According to dictionary.com, it is an optical illusion caused by atmospheric conditions. In other words, your eyes are playing tricks on you and what you see is not what you see.

What you see in front of you may be your reality, but what you believe about your reality is what changes it. A self-limiting belief is just that: a belief system that limits oneself and causes them to become stuck, stagnant, and denying change. This self-limiting belief system held me captive for years and years. Every time I would try to achieve a goal, fear would tell me that I'm not good enough or would remind me where I come from. Fear would whip up a cocktail of lies and make me drink it slowly until those lies became a part of who I believed myself to be. Fear is often referred to as "False Evidence Appearing Real" and this statement couldn't be any more true. It will make you see things that are not actual. Fear is always subject to show up in some form. When it does, it is okay to temporarily feel it, but you must know what to do.

As I began to teach my daughter how to overcome fear, I began to practice the same tactics: prayer, scripture reference, employing faith, positive affirmation, and trust in God. I would recite to the Lord that "When I'm afraid, I trust in you." I began to believe that I can and will achieve dreams and goals in my life. I began to allow my faith to rise and believe what God said about me and not what my reality said. Growth is a continuum because it's a lifelong journey.

On this journey, I have learned how to lead with uncommon courage. Prayer, using the strategy of God's Word, and submission to His will began to destroy those limiting beliefs and mindsets I once had. My process of surrender allowed me to break generational curses that won't be passed down to my children. Surrender has taught me how to lead in a way that is not common to most; as a servant.

Surrender is painful. What's more painful, though, is being paralyzed by fear and self-limiting beliefs. The good news is that beauty is on the other side of your willingness to let go of those beliefs. Here's another thing that will encourage you: God is legitimate. His Word is true and works when you put in the work. He absolutely cannot lie and when you speak His words back to Him, He hastens to perform what they say. He will strengthen you to trust Him, even in the midst of dire circumstances. He will deliver you from situations, even ones that you initiated. Hence, when your reality and fear begin to lie to you, set limits in your mind, and make you question your identity, know that it is just a mirage. Have faith and don't believe what you see. Surrender to God. Trust Him. He loves you. Selah.

Rachel Robinson

Author Bio

In a world that has multi-layered ideals about the vastness of skin representation, Rachel Robinson just wants to make sure it's healthy; a goal she has superseded with the creation of Sister and Son, LLC.

Sister and Son, LLC., is a revolutionary skincare brand infused with holistic elements and an economic uniqueness that sets it apart from all its competitors. Created with the whole person in mind, Rachel developed a formula that not only executes the clinical use of essential oils, but also champions its affordability to clients from all economic backgrounds. Rachel was given the vision from God to create Sister and Son, LLC. She aspires to consider everyone's needs by creating skincare with enough flexibility to address both the healing of dry skin and the results of facing skin challenges.

Founder Rachel Robinson attributes faith as a necessary addition in the creation of her products. Rachel has a detailed background in Interior Design and is currently earning her education in Sustainable Business- Entrepreneurship Innovation. Inspired by the need to help others overcome life's hurdles and leave a legacy of generational wealth and knowledge behind, she wishes most to fulfill God's assignment while helping people love themselves fully.

Your Story Matters

~ Canila Gist

Hey! Readers, to begin with, thank you for making the decision to purchase this book, which is full of testimonials on how to move past limitations while facing life situations. We all know this is not an easy pill to swallow. I can give you examples of many situations that I have encountered on my new journey of entrepreneurship which I officially started this year, in my late twenties.

Last year, I attended a vision board party, and this event change my whole year. The room was full of people who had desires to follow their dream, which was an eye-opener for me because I'm one of those people who like to see everyone else talk without being called upon to do the same. I strongly believe that when God is pulling on you or leading you to a particular event it's for a reason.

Last year, I went through a horrible breakup, so I was brokenhearted and lost at the same time while God pulled on my heart to attend this event. Officially in 2020, I knew this would be a new decade, a new start, and had much faith. In February, I went on my first cruise and out of the country to Jamaica, Cayman Island. While we were on the cruise, I felt God tugging on me again, and I promised myself on the cruise I would get my book project accomplished, which hasn't happened yet, but currently, I have participated in two book projects and I'm so proud of myself! I have collaborated with some really great entrepreneurial "Influential Who Win," which opened the door for me to be featured on major networks such as ABC, Fox News, People Magazine, and etc.

Y'all know everything is not peaches in cream, right? I lost $2,000 to investments, trusted people who constantly let me down, had a reduction in working hours due to COVID-19, experienced car issues, got rejected many times, etc. I ended up with a lower-paying job and had no support from the community.

As you can see, I went through different situations, but that never stopped me from achieving my dreams. I always have a compassionate heart, which is key. I have studied other entrepreneurs in their journeys and noticed they experience difficulties as well but remain focused.

I started a coaching program in July 2020 and had my first client (I love helping other people achieve their dreams, as this is exciting for me). I gave her worksheets and came up with strategic ways to assist her. We had so much fun. It gave me great joy to see she was improving! Unfortunately, someone in my past somehow connected with her. This particular individual and I had a few disagreements, but, you know, life goes on. I guessed my client had mentioned her name to her, and from there, it just went downhill. I had to start chasing my client for her session, but she ignored my calls repeatedly...

I was distraught and upset because we had made so many improvements. Previously, I had had other clients who paid and after one session dropped; nevertheless, I witnessed so many of them make improvement. I still congratulated them on the improvements and seeing the smiles on their faces made me feel fulfilled.

No matter how many times you may fail, always find a way to get back up, because success is

ALL about taking risks. Always remember, "YOU GOT THIS;" don't look to the sidelines; just stay focused.

Canila Gist

Author Bio

I am the proud founder of Your Story Matters Consultant LLC. I have received the Barack Obama Award, Upward Bound Awards at Winston- Salem State University; and participated for in The National Black Theater Festival for several years. I have been honored in 3 International Best-Selling books; to include honorable mentions in the 2020 Women Who Win feature. I've been mentored by Celebrity Coach Toney Gaskins, Min. Nakita Davis, CEO of Jesus, Coffee, and Prayer Christian Publishing House LLC., and received great Guidance from Shirley Clark & Dr. Pat Bailey. I've been interviewed by legendary, Nikki Rich (Oprah Ambassador) and collaborated with Mrs. California Tee Lee of #SHEISFoundationNetwork 2020. My speaker career includes being a Guest Speaker for Self-Care and Secure Your Own Bag Virtual international summit. In addition, I've participated as a guest speaker at The Q.U.E.E.N Xperience international summit in 2020. I've been blessed to participate in the 2020 Success Women's Conference and glean from Inspirational Speaker Les Browns, Lisa Nichols, Iyanla Vanzant, Dr. Sonja Stribling and many more.

In addition, in 2020 I became an honoree speaker for the Success Leaves CLUES global event too. I am a Motivational Coach & Speaker who Hosts the Panel Show Your Story Matters. I am a Motivational Strategist, Speaker, and Author of Your Story Matters. My Book will be coming soon in 2021. I also had the unique opportunity to Lunch my Clothing line in September 2020, Your Story Matters. I offer all-exclusive baw$e chic boutique apparel and coaching packages online.

I have had the honor of being featured in 200 + networks featured in the New York Times, Sheen Magazine, TMZ, Cosmo, People, TEDx Talk, CBS, ABC, and Fox News Affiliates.

My passion is to help people of faith who deal with traumatic experiences, domestic violence, molestation, backsliding condition, single while waiting, cope with Homelessness, being a babe in Christ, heal, forgive, rediscover their voice and so much more. I have Ten years' experience of working with youth and carry a bachelor's degree in psychology. In 2020 because I am a soul winner for Jesus Christ!

Mi Cuba, Gloria's Story!

~ Gloria Reimherr

My Country of Birth – How It Taught Me to Be Passionate About My Adoptive Country: AMERICA....USA, Land of the FREE and the Brave.....

My Country of Birth – How It Taught Me to Be Passionate About My Adoptive Country: AMERICA....USA, Land of the FREE and the Brave..... I, *Gloria Mercedez Arrojo Cabrera* (in Latin culture, both the father and mother's last names are used), was born in the year 1951 to an upper-middle-class family. My mother was a dental surgeon. I was an only child until my brother, Manuel was born in 1957.

We had a comfortable upper-middle-class lifestyle, had membership in The Copacabana Country Club (*the authentic one*), attended private schools, and had

133

a nanny, cook, and maid. My summers were spent traveling our beautiful island country visiting family, mostly with my grandfather, Fernando. Cuba has some of the most beautiful beaches combined with lush valleys, hills, and tropical vegetation. God's Country!

I enjoyed the joys of a large extended family and was taught to read and write by my great-grandmother who lived in our home. All family gatherings were held at our home. I loved this since both of my aunts, missionaries, and pastors' wives, had large families, many cousins, to play with!

On New Year's Eve, 1959, Fidel Castro led a successful overthrow of the Fulgencio Batista Government....using the "False" pretense of restoring democracy. New Year's Eve celebration at our home in Havana quickly ceased as news of Castro's takeover blasted through the airwaves.

It was a sad evening for our family, as if someone had died! And in a way, worse than that, our freedoms were soon to be eradicated...forever!

New Year of 1960 brought in some immediate and drastic changes for Cuba. And, very quickly, it became apparent to many that in order to have liberty, you had no other choice but to leave and seek asylum in the USA. During that 1st year of the revolution, some, including my parents, got wind of a clan-descent anti-Castro movement training in Central America, supported by the CIA. This turned out to be the now historical and failed debacle of the Bay of Pigs invasion that took place on April 17-19, 1961. Our family, like many others, held high hopes that this would be the catalyst that would overthrow the Castro regime and reclaim our country.

However, this attempt to overthrow Castro quickly failed; the Bay of Pigs invasion lasted three days. Failure of this was due to the planning and training conducted under the Eisenhower administration and executed under the newly elected Kennedy one.

President JFK, under the ill advice of some left lining congressmen, stopped the air and supplies back-up missions that had been promised to the Cuban fighters. This resulted in thousands being killed and captured, and many Cubans losing the hope of ever seeing a FREE Cuba. It was then that my parents made the decision to seek asylum in the USA.

In mid-May, 1961, Father packed a suitcase, and after a teary goodbye to Mom, my brother and I took a taxi to the airport and left Cuba for the USA, never to return. He had been tipped off by a friend at the office that he was on a list and would most likely be picked up, interrogated, and jailed that coming week.

My dad went straight to NOLA where he had a job waiting for him with Lone Star Cement Corporation, the company he worked for in Havana. He immediately began applying for visas for my brother and me. My mother had hers and a current passport, but my brother and I did not. In Cuba, my mother took care of getting us passports, with my grandfather's help. But the visas had to be applied in the US by someone that would sponsor us, and that job was left up to my dad in NOLA.

The process took months, since there was a mass exodus of Cubans leaving Cuba. Many upper and middle-class Cubans knew Castro's True Colors. Once my mother had our passports and visas in hand in mid-July, she went to the airport to purchase plane tickets. However, she promptly found out that she could purchase tickets for us, but NOT for herself.

Just two weeks prior, Castro had implemented a New Law that prohibited one-way travel for professionals. As a dental surgeon, the agents could not sell her a ticket. This resulted in our devising a plan that would essentially be our "tickets out of Cuba" and to our new life in the USA.

Pan American was leaving Cuba, and their last flight was on Saturday, July 26, 1961. My mom was told by Dennis Muhlenberg, the head of Pan Am in Cuba, to be at the airport at 5 a.m. with us. We would travel as part of his family. We had Pan-Am passes, passports, and visas, but no actual tickets. The plan was that he would ride in the cockpit, his wife would carry their infant daughter, my mom would carry my brother, and I could have his seat.

When their family name was called, the six of us went together to the clearance area. We underwent the traditional search of the day – physical, duffle bags (only 35lbs. per traveler). We did not know until the plane lifted, if we had been able to pull it off!

For a 10-year-old girl, this was a real-life adventure. For Mom, I realized years later, the uprooting of all that she had accomplished professionally, as well as leaving many close relatives behind, was really difficult.

For many years, I left the memory of life in Cuba in the past, not to be re-visited, but as I gained wisdom and years, I came to embrace it as a strong part of who I was. I give thanks to God for being with us on that day in 1961 as we journeyed out of Cuba to the USA.

Arriving in New Orleans, where Dad had been living since his exit in May, the search was on to find a private school that would grant me a scholarship to attend. As a Cuban refugee then, I could not attend a public school. Since Dad spoke English, he was a frequent speaker at churches and community events regarding Cuba and the impending threat of socialism/Communism.

At one of those events, we were offered a full two-year scholarship to attend my last two years of elementary school: Trinity Baptist School in Arabi, LA. Their church also adopted our family, finding an apartment with three months' paid rent, partially furnishing it, and giving a house-warming shower for my mom, to provide some of the basic needs in a home.

(Note: pictures left to right 1966 with my grandparents, 1963 with Mom and brother Manuel, 1961 with Dad at our 1st Thanksgiving Day)

Coming to the USA as a non-English-speaking person forced me to repeat the 5th grade. I wanted to speak English at home, but Mom wanted to ensure we kept our Spanish made it mandatory for us to always speak Spanish at home. This hindered her progress in learning to speak English; however, she managed well in the years following and accomplished several careers, including obtaining a Masters in Public Health.

I was almost fluent in English by the summer of 1962, and I am truly bilingual, thanks in a big way to mom. When I speak in Spanish, I think in Spanish, and the same goes for English. I can honestly say that all that I have accomplished throughout my life was influenced by the uncommon courage I witnessed growing up. My experience as a Cuban refugee influenced me to become a passionate defender of the Constitution of the USA, my adoptive Country.

God bless the United States of America!

Gloria Reimherr

Author Bio

Effective communication can be as necessary as the air we breathe. Establishing an organic connection with people; is a virtue envied by most yet attained by few. Combining a natural ability with over forty years of valued experience , Gloria Reimherr is known for her keen ability to connect with many, through the power of heartfelt communication.

Gloria Reimherr is an International Best-Selling Author, humanitarian, translator, and a marketing and promoting guru.

Bringing many years of successful communication throughout the Mississippi Gulf Coast and surrounding areas, Gloria is reputed for her exceptional skillsets, as a Spanish to English translator, interpreter, and sales and marketing specialist with GMR Marketing & More. There, she provides clients with the language and interpretation services needed, to remove possible barriers and to build a more trusted experience with the proprietor. As an independent professional, Gloria provides a myriad of both translator and interpretation services; via phone, correspondence, and various online platforms, proving her to be one *set apart* from many others in her professional field.

Gloria's Mantra is simple: Go the extra mile.

More than an exceptional professional, Gloria Reimherr is also a compassionate leader in her local community. She is currently a board member on both the **GFM - Gone Fishing Ministries and GCN - Gulf Coast Networking,** where both her service and intellectual perspectives are greatly valued. Known for her contributions in both fundraising and community service, Gloria is living out her personal mantra daily.

When Gloria is not providing excellent service both in business and in her local community, she is loved greatly by close family and friends.

Gloria Reimherr. Specialist. Leader. Servant.

Uncommon Courage

~ Alicia Galloway

*There we **saw** the giants, and we like grasshoppers in our **own sight,** and so we were in tier sight."*
Numbers 13:33

With men, this is impossible, but all things are possible with God. Matthew 19:26

I know that you can do all things and no thoughts or purpose of yours can be thwarted (prevented from being accomplished.) Job 42:2

Do you have a lifelong dream, passion, or desire that has yet to manifest? What is the most internal desire of your heart that constitutes success? Now, close your eyes and visualize it coming to pass. Would you like to see them come to fruition in real life? If so, what is hindering your success? How do you **see** yourself?

How do you **see** the obstacles that are preventing your success? Are your thinking patterns limiting your success?

I'm not good enough. I don't have time. I'm not educated enough. I'm not creative. I have children. I'm too old. It's too big to accomplish. I don't have enough experience. I'm too young. No one will want what I have to offer. I'm going to fail.

Have you allowed any of these perceptions to become your anthem song hindering the very dreams, desires, and passions that you visualized coming to pass? If so, it is time to change the way that **you** currently **see** and focus on the way **God sees**. In fact, God sees you as a winner, an adequate person, unique, an overcomer, and more than a conqueror (2 Timothy 3:17, 1 John 5:4, Romans 8:37, 1 Peter 2:9, Ps. 139:14, Ps. 29:11).

In Numbers 14, the Israelites faced obstacles in the form of literal giants that hindered them from entering Canaan, the Promised Land flowing with milk and honey that God promised to Abraham. Following the Lord's instruction regarding the land He gave to them, Moses sent Caleb, Joshua, and ten other men to scout the land of Canaan and bring back a report of what they **saw**. Upon their return, the ten spies reported **seeing** land with abundant fruit, land that devours its inhabitants, and land with giants that would be impossible to defeat. As they faced the giants, they began to **see** themselves as grasshoppers. However, scouting the same land, Caleb and Jacob provided a different report of what they **saw**. They were able to **see** Canaan as a land that could be conquered and possessed.

When facing the giants hindering your success, who do you currently identify with most? Jacob and Caleb, or the ten spies? Do you **see** yourself as a grasshopper fighting giants or do you **see** God? The ten spies failed to **see** themselves as the same children of God Whom He brought out of Egypt, Who guided them in the wilderness in the form of a cloud by day and a pillar of fire by night, and as Jehovah Jireh, Who made food provisions for them in the form of manna that rained from the sky and quail that came in from the sea!. They chose to focus on their weaknesses and what they were able to accomplish in their own human strength instead of God's supernatural strength and abilities. Their limited perceptions as grasshoppers and their failure to **see** past the giants caused their dreams to be unfulfilled as they weren't able to enter into the land of Canaan that flowed with fruit, milk, and honey (Ex. 14:23).

Contrarily, Caleb and Joshua followed God fully and believed that He would take care of the giants resulting in the fulfillment and success of possessing the land of Canaan for Caleb and his descendants (Ex. 14:24). Be determined (today) to **see** God's supernatural ability and believe the giants in the way of your success can and will be slain.

For the vision (*dream*) is yet for the appointed [future] time. It hurries toward the goal [of fulfillment]; it will

144

not fail. Even though it delays, wait [patiently] for it, because it will certainly come; it will not delay. (Habakkuk 2:2-3)

At the golden age of twenty, I was a newly married military wife, honorably discharged from the military, a new mother, far away from home at a new duty station, working full-time at a place unaligned with my desires, and with an unfinished college degree. Additionally, as some of you may relate, I also did the cooking, cleaning, feeding, diaper changing, and grocery shopping--everything! Growing up, I had a dream to obtain a degree in education. I desired the Proverb 31 Virtuous Woman example of success. However, I had unknowingly become a grasshopper fighting giants. The perceptions that had become my anthem song included: "I can't do this because I have a child," "I have no support," "How will I pay for this?" and "I don't have time."

After seeking the word of the Lord, He illuminated two scriptures (Mathew 19:26 & Job 42:2-*listed under title*) that caused me to no longer see myself as a grasshopper fighting giants of fear and doubt. Instead, I was able to see Him as my Victory and Waymaker. He miraculously opened the door for me to become a Teacher's Assistant that, in turn, provided me with the time and platform needed to complete my Bachelor's degree. I even received funding for my tuition! Had I focused on what I couldn't do as a grasshopper in my own sight, I would have never obtained a degree. I now have two degrees and I'm currently working on my Doctorate!

By seeing God, we can R.I.S.E our way to success. **Realize** you serve a God Who wants to fulfill the desires of your heart (Ps.37:4). **Initialize** a God-inspired plan to accomplish your dreams and goals. **Supersize** God, not your giants, as you stand and declare His word daily. **Externalize** what you initialized by stepping out on faith and preparing for your future testimony of success. Don't limit yourself by focusing on what you can't do. Instead, focus on what our limitless God can do.

Alicia Galloway

Author Bio

"God is within her, she will not fail. She is clothed with strength and dignity." (Ps. 46:5; Prov. 31:25)

Alicia Galloway was born and raised in the Mississippi Gulf Coast area, the place where you go in for a handshake and get a hug! She is currently married with three sons in the Atlanta metro area. Alicia is a results-oriented and data-driven educational leader with a history of success in driving strategies, programs, and initiatives that have promoted academic excellence, achievement, and continuous school improvement. She is passionate about Christian living, discipleship, and imparting the word of God to others. Alicia considers her faith, family, and friends to be most important to her. Just as her favorite author, John Bevere, she is determined to live a life that counts today and forever by being driven by eternity.

Living in the Shadows

~ **Suzanne Packard**

But then I had this sweet pulling in my heart to follow and want more of God, to inspect, to grasp the deep penetration of His love for me that I could not imagine or fathom, but desired. He says to open myself to His loving Presence so that He can fill me with His fullness. He wants us to experience how wide, deep, long, and high His love is for us, which is inconceivable to me, but I desire it all the same, and crave more of it. But I'm getting ahead of myself.

At one point in my life, I felt so very alone and angry at God who took my brother at the young age of 19 from a motorcycle accident. It was the summer between my junior and senior year of high school. I was madly in love with my boyfriend of 2 years, and he had asked me to marry him 2 months prior, but that all changed with my brother's death. My only other sibling was 9 years older than me and living in a different town. The devastation of my brother's death left me not only without a brother, but also my parent's marriage suffered, and I was left to fend for my life, and I didn't know how to proceed, through the grief, bitterness, anger, and the depression, so I turned to drugs, skipping school, failing classes, and breaking up with my boyfriend.

I did manage to graduate high school and started getting back on track with my life of going to nursing school, but then several events happened. I was rear ended twice, and I was in a car accident that totaled my car and started dating a guy who was much older and going through a divorce. I didn't see this at the time of me being the rebound of someone he was still in love with, and I found myself pregnant while still in nursing school with his baby. The struggles of not knowing what to do at a young age I was convinced by my boyfriend to have an abortion. I had no idea of how it would affect me afterwards, but I was numb to the world walking around like a zombie, but managed to graduate from nursing school, and get a job. By then I was living with my boyfriend and hoping he would ask me to marry him soon, as I thought we both were in love, and that's when I found myself pregnant again and struggling with how to respond to his request of wanting me to have another abortion. I think I was so dazed in love with him, and numb from having my first abortion that I agreed to his suggestion, but soon found out he was having an affair with someone else, and I was suffering the consequences of 2 abortions.

I had deep depression and suicidal suggestions in my mind; in fact, my mind never stopped accusing me of the abortions which led me into drinking and at times drugs to get rid of the thoughts, but that just exacerbated them of so much guilt, shame and lies to family and friends. At one point I got very bold and told a family member about my abortions so that we could bond more, but I was told God was never going to forgive me and I was going to hell for what I did.

Years later I found out the truth that God loves me and forgives me and sent His Son to die on the cross for me. Today, I can testify of that deep love the Lord has for me, and I am no longer living in the shadows, but in freedom from my past and the voices in my mind. I was able to get that freedom through the Lord and the mercy and grace of my mentors, teachings from small groups, faith-based conferences, and various Pastors' teachings.

The Lord said that He would always take care of me, but in the beginning of my walk with Him, it was difficult to believe because of my past. One of the first desires I had was to go on a mission trip to Mexico with my church, but for some reason, I chickened out at the last minute, and my Pastor kept saying after they got back, "I should have gone; I missed out." As crazy as it sounds, I found scripture one morning that was releasing me from my work at the family practice, and I put in my 2-week notice. Everyone kept asking me what I was going to do for employment, but I didn't know. Then I decided to volunteer at the Women's

Resource Center, and when I walked through the door, they told me they had been praying for me to come there.

Two months after arriving the current nurse left unexpectedly and I was asked to apply for the job as the nurse manager helping women in my community with unplanned pregnancies. I have had the privilege to tell my testimony for the past 13 years and to show them through an ultrasound what their baby looks like and to hear their heartbeat for the very first time. Besides the multiple healing studies that I have participated in the most profound and enlightening was the Post Abortion Healing Study that threw off the weight of my guilt and shame of my abortions, and now I have the privilege of leading this group yearly to help other women who are struggling with their abortions. *It never ceases to amaze me all that God has done through my life in helping others to heal and love again.*

Suzanne Packard

Author Bio

Suzanne Packard is a Licensed Practical Nurse with over 40 years of experience in combined areas of surgery, ENT, Family Practice, Home Health, Ortho-Neuro, Labor/Delivery, but for the past 13 years has been the Nurse Manager at the Women's Resource Center. There she performs ultrasounds and presents a post-abortion healing study for women who are struggling with a past abortion and it's emotional, physical, relational, and spiritual effects.

Although Suzanne was born and raised in Minneapolis, Minnesota, and has lived in several states for the past 25 years, she currently resides on the Mississippi Gulf Coast and enjoys spending time with her children and grandchildren.

Worthy

~ Becky Farrell

"You are precious in my sight. You are honored, and I love you!" Isaiah 43:4

Today, I know these things! However, my mind drowned in deceit for decades. At the very core was the fundamental belief that I was unworthy. This flawed belief developed at a very young age due to the toxic environment I was forced to grow up in.

Life was wonderful and charmed growing up in the care of my grandparents! That all changed and my heart was shattered into a million little pieces when my parents suddenly and without warning took me away at the young age of five. I was so confused. I cried for days. Those days of tears rolled into days, months, years, decades.

As a result, of my parents decision I formed many negative beliefs about who and what I was. Perhaps, because I was separated from my baby sister. Maybe, it was because I longed for the safety of my bedroom, my toys, and the unconditional love of my grandparents. Mostly, back then I was in shock and perplexed at why no one, including God, rescued me. My mind and heart were both broken.

So, at a very tender age, I vowed to build a different life than the one my parents chose to live. I vowed to make something of myself. I vowed to be in a home that offered safe refuge!

Growing up with my parents was a challenge to say to least. Nonetheless, I got myself up and went to school every day. School became my refuge. Books were my escape. I studied hard and excelled academically.

As a teenager, I worked odd jobs saving as much money as I could. At the tender age of 15, I left home to escape abuse. 15 years old is way too young to adult. I made many bad choices and paid a heavy cost.

Still, I went on to be the first person in my family to graduate high school. In my Junior year I fell in love. I married him in my Senior year. We had two children, a boy and girl. Fortunately, I raised two amazing children who are incredible adults now.

I landed a great job dental assisting after graduation, which gave me the skill to maintain steady employment. Despite my accomplishments, at my very core was the fundamental belief that I was unworthy.

This mindset polluted all my relationships, including my relationship with God. By 25, I was a divorced single mom struggling to support my precious little family. Fortunately, my children and I were able to move in with my grandfather while they were still young. There, I was able to further my education. I went on to college and law school. I graduated at the top of my class.

Unfortunately, even this tremendous feat was not enough to defeat my sense of unworthiness. Still, because my grandparents kept me in Church, I had deep faith in God and His love carried me through very tough times. Eventually, I opened a law firm and began a blessed career.

However, no matter, what I did there was always that sense of unworthiness at my core. It permeated all areas of my life, the ability to be loved, to love, to forgive, and to breathe.

But God! One day God's love broke through! I know now that He was chasing me and protecting me all my life. But, until this day, His love alluded me.

Then, the barriers in my mind washed away listening to the radio. It was a beautiful sunny day. There I was driving down the gulf coast along the beach. The song REDEEMED by Big Daddy Weave was playin. Those who know me understand that I love music and it's always blaring on my radio! That day! That time! That moment! Big Daddy's lyrics permeated my soul. I pulled over on the white sandy beach and began to sob like a baby. The tears were those buried by that little five-year-old abandoned girl. God. caught. Every. One. of them. I must have played it over a 100 times. All the while sobbing! "All my life I have been called unworthy." Yes Lord, Yes!

"I've got a new life. A new name. I am not the same. Thank God, redeemed." I heard God say, Becky I want you! Find me! I Am Here!

So, I immediately joined a non-denominational church and got into a small group. I desperately wanted the freedom that Big Daddy expounded! And I chased it like the plaque!

Before joining that Church, I had begun experiencing small tastes of freedom. My sunshine angel daughter introduced me to Christian music, and I began believing in a kind loving God. Still, I held on too many self-limiting beliefs that were deeply ingrained.

Until, one fateful night, when all my chains were broken. That night, our FREEDOM small group leaders, Dorothy Wilson and Tiffany Denise Bell assigned a life-changing activity where they asked us to write down a number from one to ten. The scale represented how each one of us thought God saw us. One represented the worst spiritual condition of our lives and ten represented perfection in God's sight.

Well, darn I struggled. It was so hard not to write a one or two. That was the unworthiness! I hesitantly wrote a tiny number five, the safe place right in the middle.

Surely, I couldn't go wrong there. I so wanted to please my leaders. Then, Dorothy went around the room and asked us to reveal our numbers and explain our responses. No one wrote 10! When it got to me, I explained, "I am a five, because I have been working really hard and hitting the mark more now than ever." Wrong. We were all wrong.

Tiffany had us turn the page over and write a ten. "What? No way," I said to myself. But, she explained, "You are all wrong. Because of Christ, God sees you as a ten!" *WAIT, what?! Hold the phone! What did you just say?*

Dorothy and Tiffany eloquently explained that because Jesus' blood washed me clean, I was a TEN! I was worthy! For me, she explained that no matter what I do or what I fail to do, I am a ten in God's presence because of Christ.

I began to sob. She said that my actions cannot and will not make me a ten; it is what Christ did for me on the cross that defines me (Eph 2:9). I don't need a marriage, a degree, or any other worldly accomplishment to stand on because my true worth is in Christ alone. On that rock I stand!

Wow, for decades I exhaustingly chased after something that was freely available to me all along. I was prayed over that night! And if you've ever been prayed over by Dorothy, Tiffany and a group of Godly women you know it is life changing!

Instantly, that scared little five-year-old girl felt truly loved for the first time in 50 years! I COULD BREATHE! I COULD APPROACH GOD! I WAS WORTHY! BECAUSE OF MY JESUS, I AM WORTHY!

In conclusion, self-limiting mindsets are not easily overcome. Yet, conquering them is absolutely necessary to having an abundant and victorious LIFE. Surround yourself with Godly women! Plant yourself in a life giving Church! Seek God! Keep seeking. Keep praying. Keep trudging.

Avail yourself of each and every avenue you can for help! Keep Surrounding yourself with Godly people that speak life into you. READ AND STUDY YOUR BIBLE.

HIs Word will permeate your soul and transform your life. When you learn to see yourself as God sees you, EVERYTHING WILL CHANGE!

Be blessed. Child of God, He is there waiting for you! JUMP, because you are a TEN! You are Worthy! And You are Precious in His sight!

Becky Farrell

Author Bio

Becky Mae Alien Farrell is a Child of God, mother, grandmother, attorney and entrepreneur. She practices law in the quaint little beach town of Bay St. Louis, MS. Her firm's clients include those injured in truck, boat, bike, and car accidents. She practices general law and handles estate planning and probate, pre-marital planning, divorce, and criminal defense.

Mrs. Farrell is active in the legal community and her professional organizations include the MS Bar Assc, the Hancock County Bar Assc, and she is a LJAP volunteer. She is a fierce advocate for those in her profession struggling with depression or mental health issues. Mrs. Farrell is an active member and Director of Children and youth ministry at Shoreline Park Baptist Church, Zone Chair for Lions Club of SO MS, and Past President and Treasurer for Bay St. Louis Lions Club. She serves on the boards of many local nonprofit organizations.

Her awards include 2020 Top 10 Criminal Defense Attorney in Mississippi, 2019 MS Gulf Coast Top Influencer, 2019 Women of Achievement Award, and MARTINDALE-HUBBELL Client Champion Gold.

Beauty from Ashes

~ Cristina Yanes

It was a busy weekend; my son and I went to a restaurant to celebrate with some of our closest friends the most important day of their lives. Everything was fine, until we started heading back home and it suddenly happened; a deep pressure in my chest, I have never experienced something like that, a pressure, a fear, all at once; everything started to escalate inside me.

I was not alone; my son was there and the fear grew worse. I began imagining him being alone and unprotected. What if something happens to me? My heart was beating fast. We walked to the car and I turned on some music to have a distraction from my own thoughts. Our home was close, just 20 minutes from there; not a long distance, but I felt each minute as an eternity.

My heart was beating faster, the fear was overtaking my body even more, my breathing was unsteady, and I felt like I could not breathe. My hands were shaking; my body and my legs were numb. Inside my mind, I was fainting. I knew I needed the strength to drive to a safe place. The silence was uncomfortable; I could not feel the air moving. Nothing was enough. I started looking around, trying to find help. I grabbed my cellphone and called my mom. She was talking to me and trying to calm me, but nothing was enough. I was completely sure that I was dying, with no one coming to rescue me. I was going to die, leaving my sons alone with two losses in less than a month. Their father died after fighting against brain cancer that March and now I was going to die with an unidentified diagnostic (Panic Attack).

Then the battlefield in my mind started. The only important things were my sons, so I thought I couldn't die; they needed me! Many thoughts were coming and going. I ended up at the ER. I had to decide if I was going to let these thoughts control my life. Was I going to be admitted into a mental facility away from my sons? No, I was not; I was going to fight this, fight for my kids, fight for myself, fight for my dreams. My mental response would determine the path of my life. I recognized that I had to have grit, drive, an internal motor to push me to get better, to be better, to heal, to grow, to grieve.

You never know what life has for you. You never know what challenges will come to you. You never know how you are going to overcome them and what is coming next. But you do know that no matter what challenges, fears, trials come your way you are going to overcome them! No matter how deep you go there is always a way out. Trust me, I have been there, and I have touched the bottom, but I stood up and overcame not only my fears, my anxiety, and depression, but also I am fulfilling my dreams.

You are never prepared for what is coming; you might think you are, but you are not. I was not prepared to lose my husband, Hentzel. If anyone asked me, we were going to win the battle of cancer and things will go back to normal. We did! We won the battle with the *ultimate healing* and he won heaven as his new home.

Fear started growing in me after his death. The biggest fear was being alone, raising my boys, and knowing that I cannot die, I should not, but how can you be in control of that when you just learned that time does not depend on you?

Grieving, making decisions, raising my kids, and being strong for them was not easy. The root of my fears was leaving my sons alone but the motor that pushed me out of my pain, my anxiety, and depression were also them. I did not heal from one day to another. I had to learn day-by-day, hour-by-hour. To be honest, I am still healing and learning.

My boys were my determination. I left that emergency room dazed, sedated by the administration of strong medicine and confused; I knew that a difficult journey was coming ahead; I could see that it was not going to be easy, but I was determined to do it for my boys and for myself.

"I am not longer a slave of fear, I am a child of God." (Bethel Worship). I repeated that phrase several times looking at myself in the mirror, but was not really believing those words. I was right there with my anxiety enslaving me, shaking and living in fear, but I repeated it again and again for several days until I gained strength, and one day the fear was gone.

God does not want us to live in fear. *"God gave us a spirit not of fear but of power, love and self-control." 2 Timothy 1:7.* His promises are real, and His Word is alive.

I had a support group; my closest friends and my church family were supporting me with prayers and fighting this battle with me. I had friends praying for me on the phone, others staying with me on my bad days, and others just encouraging me during this process. Prayers, bible verses, and worship songs allowed my fears to be pushed away little by little.

Healing took place in many ways. I wanted to give my sons the best of me. I started living again, setting goals and living every day, as it will be my last one. My relationship with God was unique; I knew He was holding me. During those days when I was feeling down, with anxiety trying to win the battle, He was taking care of me, reminding me of His love and who I was. He was there, I was not alone, and He was not going to let me go downhill. I could feel that; He was going to bless me.

I love to remember how God touched my life. I was broken, my life was in ashes, but He took care of me and brought beauty from ashes. Years have passed, and God has taken care of my boys and me in so many ways.

Financially? He has provided.
Emotionally? He has healed.
Physically? He has restored.

My boys are teenagers now. God has provided a male role model every day since their dad died; our church family has always been there for us. In His promises, He said He was going to restore our lives, *"Beauty from Ashes."*

I remarried in 2019 to a wonderful man who loves my boys as his own; he is an answered prayer that surpassed all my expectations. Believe me, I prayed a long list of characteristics for the man that was going to be part of our family. God heard my prayers and took care of every single detail.

Not only did He give us a husband that loves us, but also He put a purpose and a dream in my life, which is to help women to overcome their fears and believe in themselves. I want to see them develop as leaders that will make a difference in the community.

Fight your battle, but do not fight it alone. Do not stay quiet; get people to support you, to listen to your fears, to encourage you. We all are fighters, and when we put the *Greatest Warrior* on our side, He will fight the battle for you. Remember, He brings beauty from ashes!

"The Lord will fight for you; you need only to be still."
Exodus 14:14

"The Lord Himself goes before you and will be with you; he will never leave you nor forsake you. Do not be afraid; do not be discouraged." Deuteronomy 31:8.

Cristina Yanes

Author Bio

Cristina Yanes is the assistant director of the Women's Resource Center. She was born and raised in Quito, Ecuador. At the age of 18, she moved to the United States adopting Mississippi as her home. After serving many years at church, Cristina transitioned to Team Coordinator at her husband's church, where she has the opportunity to serve the Hispanic Community. She believes in encouraging women and empowering them to reach their dreams.

Cristina has two energetic teenagers, Benjamin, 13, and Mathias, 12. Recently, she remarried Harim Yanes, Associate Pastor at Roca Sólida Church, and owner of Yanes Plus Lawn Care Company. Cristina's passion is to help others lead and grow in every aspect of their lives and to show them that even in the darkest place, there is a light that will bring back hope.

Being a Victim of Bullying
Made Me a Caring Teacher

~ **Brenda Anita Swayer**

I like to say that I come from "humble beginnings," where I grew up in the New York City housing projects and attended the New York City public school system. I was happy that I came from a "closely knit" Christian family, where we always attended church and went everywhere together as a family. I was brought up in the Baptist church where I was taught to love God and His people. Not only did the church teach me this, so did my parents. They taught me the values and morals for respecting others. Unfortunately, some of my peers and even some of my teachers did not reciprocate the same respect to me. A few of my teachers even called me and the other students names and said we were not smart enough to get jobs. As a child, this type of ridicule came as a shock to me because I thought my African-American teachers were supposed to build up my self-esteem. In retrospect, that was really considered a form of adult bullying.

However, for the most part my classmates and I got along well with each other, for the exception of Jean, Ema, and Mary who always started fights with me. It was to no avail trying to make friends with them, no matter how hard I tried. They just did not like me for some reason. Jean, the ringleader, would constantly try to start fights with me before, during, and after school. During school, Jean would step all over my new shoes, push me down, and tell Mary to take my lunch money from me. They would dare me to tell my teacher Mrs. Farrow, because they would beat me up after school if I did. Of course, I was afraid of the afterschool repercussions, so I never told Mrs. Farrow.

Whether I told Mrs. Farrow or not, there were still afterschool repercussions where the three girls jumped me while I was walking home from school. The bullying happened consistently from third grade to fifth grade. I remember going home crying and telling my parents I never wanted to return to school. Naturally, my parents were quite concerned and decided to meet with the girls' parents to discuss the matter. After the discussion, the bullying subsided for about two weeks, then started right back up. At this point, my parents advised me to ignore the girls and if it continued happening, to bring it to the attention of Mrs. Farrow. When the bullying started happening again, I had no other choice but to tell Mrs. Farrow. However, much to my astonishment, Mrs. Farrow just gave me a stern look and told me to sit down. She did absolutely nothing to resolve the issue. By now my parents were livid and decided to discuss my situation with the school principal, Mrs. Tucker. Her response was, "We don't allow this type of behavior in our school and you know, kids will be kids." Now, was I missing something here? I know there was clearly an "elephant in the room," but no one wanted to address it.

I can remember asking myself what I did to deserve such unfair treatment. I started feeling as if I wasn't good enough to fit in anywhere. Being a Christian, I always believed in the power of prayer, so one night I prayed and asked God to forgive Jean, Ema, and Mary and to protect me from being bullied by them. Yes, God answered my prayers, because by the end of the fifth grade school year, the bullying gradually stopped. As we began maturing and getting ready to enter Middle School, the same girls who were my bullies wanted to become my friend. Interestingly enough, we found out that we had so much more in common than we knew. That was only God! I knew then that God had a much greater plan for my life. Jeremiah 29:11 lets me know that God's plans are of peace and not of evil, to give me an expected end. Now, I was ready to expect my end and it didn't matter what others said or thought about me, because I knew who I was in Christ. I knew that I could do all things through Christ who strengthened me. Philippians 4:13

I became that overcomer, that survivor, that caring and nurturing teacher I aspired to be at the age of five. My love for children and teaching became my passion. I knew the importance of discipline, being fair, and implementing "conflict resolution" in my classroom.

Whenever my students encountered problems with each other, I never ignored them by "sweeping them under the carpet" like my teacher Mrs. Farrow did. I would address the issues of my students, while working closely with their parents to resolve reoccurring issues. My mission was to be the best teacher God had called me to be. The call on my life made me stand out from the rest and stand strong in my conviction. I genuinely cared about each one of my students and tried to be there whenever they needed someone to talk to. I taught from a heart filled with love and respect and made an indelible impact on each student's life. I wanted to provide my students with a family environment which I believe was conducive to learning. Some of my now adult students still keep in contact with me because of the mutual love and respect we have for each other.

I truly do believe that God allowed me to experience elementary school bullying to strengthen and prepare me to become the best teacher I could possibly be. I thank God that my parents instilled in me to be the best and raised me up to be that strong person I am today

"Train up a child in the way he should go: and when he is old, he will not depart from it." Proverbs 22:6

Brenda Sawyer

Author Bio

Educators are the quintessential underpinning of the world. Without their contributions to society, we would be void of any form of evolution. Amongst many, making the world a better place to learn in, Brenda Sawyer is an intricate piece of the educational structure.

Brenda Sawyer is a Best-Selling Author, educator, and **CEO of GIRLS WALKING WITH INTEGRITY EMPOWERING FOR DESTINY (GWWI)®**

Having spent over 26 years as an elementary school teacher in the Philadelphia School System, Brenda has strong reputation for bringing integrity, credibility, and professional knowledge to a myriad of educational constructs.

Her intention is clear: *to remain as one known for bridging the gap of communication between the generations.*

Meeting intention with undeniable action, diligence, and impartation, Brenda Sawyer has met the demands of a shifting culture, with reliability and servant leadership. **GIRLS WALKING WITH INTEGRITY EMPOWERING FOR DESTINY (GWWI)®,** by which Brenda is both Founder and CEO, is a Christian Mentoring Ministry that empowers and encourages young ladies between the ages of eight and eighteen to make a transformation in their lives through biblical principles and teaching. Born from within its cause, she also published Encouraging

Words For The Mind, Spirit And Soul, a collection of devotions taken from **GIRLS WALKING WITH INTEGRITY EMPOWERING FOR DESTINY (GWWI)®** A book she believes triggered a spirit of exhortation within her, causing her to search out biblical truths; using them as the foundation of her mentorship program.

No stranger to the respect for higher education, Brenda Sawyer holds two Masters Degrees in Elementary Education from Cabrini College and has since retired from an outstanding career in teaching.

One of her most memorable educational accomplishments includes teaching elementary students Spanish for over thirteen years. When she is not out transforming lives, Brenda remains inspired by people and the acquisition of fundamental knowledge. In all that she does, Brenda is determined to remain a woman always led by God.

Brenda Sawyer. Educator. Exhorter. Servant Leader.

Conquering a Self-Limiting Mindset of Low Self-Esteem

~ Dr. Stacy L. Henderson

A self-limiting mindset that I had to conquer was low self-esteem, because of being sexually abused as a child. I was confused about love, emotions, affection, and my body image. It was not until after I was married that I realized I was not healed from the traumas of my past. I felt ineffective as a Wife and I felt like a failure as a Mother. I was unable to effectively communicate my inner feelings because I was not equipped with the words. Thus, I became silent. Not only did I lose my voice, but also, I lost out on love, my connection with my family...I even lost myself. The aftermath of my painful realization thrust me into a downward spiral with no end in sight. Psalm 27:13-14 led me to look to God to answer my prayers and the questions about the turmoil I endured. *"I would have despaired unless I had believed that I would see the goodness of the Lord In the land of the living. Wait for the Lord. Be strong and let your heart take courage. Yes, wait for the Lord."*

Prayer, counseling, and meditation on the Word of God endowed me with the inspiration to change my thoughts and beliefs. Gradually, I began to - not only *believe* in love again - but I *found* love again. It was in the reflection of a shattered mirror of mine, a broken one from my childhood. I was looking at old photos and reminiscing over the items in my Hope Chest which I had not opened in decades. I was surprised to find that I still had that old mirror after all those years. And, when I investigated it, I saw a broken image of my frightened inner child. From that day forward, I have made it a point to occasionally glance into that mirror as a reminder - not of my shattered childhood innocence - but as a symbol of hope. The words of 1 John 4:16-18 ignited my spirit and reminded me that the love of God drives out fear. *"16 And so we know and rely on the love God has for us. God is love. Whoever lives in love lives in God, and God in them. 17 This is how love is made complete among us so that we will have confidence on the day of judgment: In this world we are like Jesus. 18 There is no fear in love. But perfect love drives out fear, because fear has to do with punishment. The one who fears is not made perfect in love."*

The Holy Spirit guided me on the path of increasing my faith and putting it into action. I knew that God *could* heal me, yet I had not shown Him that I believed that He *would* heal me. In my private times with the Lord, I sought His comfort, strength, revelation, and love. I hesitantly, but honestly, admitted to Him the insecurities that plagued me. I admitted my faults, fears, shame, and doubts. I stood before Him vulnerable in my truth - to better understand the truth He would reveal. And although I was broken-hearted and lowly in spirit, He showered me with mercy and grace. He loved me. The overflowing of the abundance of compassion God pours upon me leaves me consumed with a sense of power difficult to describe. A self-affirmation that reassures me of my abilities is Philippians 4:13: *"I can do all things through Christ who strengthens me."* Through my submission and faith in God, I am able to conquer my insecurities, overcome low self-esteem, and defeat self-doubt.

Healing from the wounds of my past is challenging, but it is worth it. It was difficult at times to acknowledge my *own* faults before I could truly walk down the road to recovery. I needed to be forgiven for the negative thoughts and actions which led to self-inflicted wounds of insecurity. There were times that I doubted God's love for me and was unclear of His compassion. I allowed the naysayers who shunned me to influence me in a harmful way. Once I started recovering, I started rethinking. My thought processes were renewed, and my spirit was refreshed. A huge part of my recovery was my redirection to the truth: God's truth. So, not only did I seek God's forgiveness...I sought self-forgiveness as well. I needed to come to the full realization that my shortcomings as a human being rendered me unworthy and imperfect. But by the Grace of God, I am made perfect through Christ Jesus. Healing hurts, but the pain is necessary to break through - rather than break down. The words of Isaiah 41:10 reminds me that God is with us, through good and bad times, and we must go forward, relying on Him every step of the way. *"Fear thou not; for I am with thee: be not dismayed; for I am thy God: I will strengthen thee; yea, I will help thee; yea, I will uphold thee with the right hand of my righteousness."*

God is masterful in His dealings with His people. No matter the trials of tribulations I have endured in my life, I am ever sure that God has a plan and a divine purpose for me, as confirmed by Jeremiah 29:11. And with Kingdom Authority, I walk boldly in my purpose. Only God could take an abused, soiled, damaged and broken young girl and transform her into a Proverbs 31 Woman. Each day my mirror's reflection shows me as I truly am - renewed, refreshed, refined, and restored. And, when there are times that I second-guess myself or seem unsure, I find myself reciting the words of Proverbs 3:5-6: *"5 Trust in the Lord with all thine heart; and lean not unto thine own understanding. 6 In all thy ways acknowledge him, and he shall direct thy paths."* To God be the Glory!

Dr. Stacy L. Henderson

Author Bio

Dr. Stacy L. Henderson, a native of Savannah, Georgia, is a highly decorated retired Naval Officer with over 25 years of military service and experience. She is a Christian Educator, Inspirational Speaker, Businesswoman and an International Best-Selling Author - with two publications in the White House Library. Her *Stacy's Stocking Stuffers* Christmas Charity has provided toys, meals, coats, clothing and monetary support for families around the world since 1991.

Stacy has spent much of her life overcoming challenges. Her *Survival Journal* chronicles her trauma and triumph over childhood sexual assault and domestic abuse as an adult. In it, she shares first-hand accounts while raising awareness of domestic violence. Her personal story of triumph over tragedy was featured in multiple other Media Outlets. With violence on the rise among our youth, she also provides age-appropriate anti-bullying training to young adults. She testified at Congressional Hearings in efforts to get tougher abuse perpetrator laws passed during the President Clinton and President Obama Administrations. She is an active member of the National Coalition Against Domestic Violence (NCADV).

Her Professional Affiliations include: National Baptist Convention, USA, Inc.; Gullah Geechee Sea Island Coalition; *Spirit of Excellence* Business Awards (Stellar Productions); 'Toots for Books' Literacy Foundation; Professional Woman Network; National Women Veterans United; Veterans of Foreign Wars; Frank

Callen Boys and Girls Club; and Delta Sigma Theta Sorority, Inc. Her personal accolades include Outstanding Georgia Citizen, Chicago Defender *Woman of Excellence*, BET *Her* Humanitarian, Reaching Back Foundation Phenomenal Woman, NCADV *Power Up, Survivor Activist, Queen Xperience Woman of Influence,* Two (2) Guinness World Records, "Keys to the City" for Eight (8) United States locales and countless other Military and Civilian Awards and Commendations.

Stacy shares her life experiences and relies on faith-based doctrines to motivate and inspire others to achieve their best mental, physical and spiritual health. A Proverbs 31 Woman, she utilizes her Spiritual Gifts to glorify God and edify His people. She is a devoted wife, proud mother of two adult children, KeiSha and William, and a doting grandmother - blessed to be members of a beautiful 'Blended and Extended' Family. They are active in their church and community. To God be the Glory!

Take the Limits Off

~ **Ashley Johnson**

"Get Up! Ashley, Get Up! Get up off of the floor and never allow yourself or anyone else to bring you to this point again." That still small voice of God has a funny way of displaying His grace. That day, He had poured His grace out on me like a never-ending river. I had allowed beliefs of myself and what others had to say about who they thought I should be, to bring me to my lowest of lows. The voices of "You'll never lose the weight"; "You're not well-versed enough"; "They'll never listen to your content and never buy your brand"; and the oldie but goody "You're not pretty enough" had overtaken my views of myself. I had splurged on many expensive conferences, created, and recited affirmations, and kept all the encouraging podcasts playing in my ears, yet I lay on the floor empty. I had quit on myself in so many life endeavors over the years and I was okay with quitting on myself to the point of death. And so I attempted.

Then the Spirit of the Lord spoke to me, loud and clear. So, as I obeyed, my body began to rid itself of the pills previously taken to end it all. I wiped the tears from my face and chose the new path ahead of me. It was the path of healing. Step by step, day by day, I chose each voice to tackle and dug deep to find the why. Why was I allowing self-sabotage through these voices? The more I became honest with myself, the more I realized I had work to do. I was allowing the spirit of fear to rule my life in every aspect. I was afraid to allow myself to really be successful, and to come into my purpose. I was afraid of the rejection that comes with being successful as well. I had seen people serve in their purpose and then die. (As if life just somehow ends when you begin serving in your purpose.) I knew, in order to deal with the spirit of fear, you have to first recognize it and want to get rid of it.

Another thing I knew was that fear could not touch the success I had already experienced. I knew that before this low place, everything that I had put my hands to had been blessed. Being the self-reflector that I am, I began to ask myself, "How do I define success?" You see, success in society is not always success to the individual experiencing it. We set goals, reach them, and still want more. What did this "more" look like for me? What was it going to take to break the self-limiting beliefs?

Trusting myself. Trusting who God created me to be was the answer. In the past, I always doubted how great my designs really were, despite all the good reviews. One day, a Facebook memory post of a picture of a bride I had previously designed for popped up on my phone. I found myself in shock, like always, at how amazing my designs had been. I went through more posts from the past, printed out other achievements, and pasted them on a small poster board to keep before me. This was an encouraging yet weird way to wake myself up. God knew that's what I needed to keep the process of healing going. I also had to keep it real with my closest friends and have honest conversations with them. I was able to tell them my hidden struggles and they began encouraging me and reminding me of who they knew me to be, and of the talents I forgot I had.

The strength I've always carried to become the butterfly I was set to be in the seasons to come was unfolding. The final step to my process was one of the hardest. I had to begin standing up for myself to family members that felt that they could speak to me any kind of way just because we were related by blood. As I spoke up for myself, the more some of my family made it feel that they no longer supported me. Little did I know, as their support fell off, strangers' support picked up. People were seeing a change in me. They saw the consistency, the drive, the confidence that was exuded through all my social media posts.

Every day, I chose to be consistent, fight through not feeling up for the challenge of being a better me until it flowed. I no longer cared about people's opinions of me and they were none of my business. Those self-limiting voices that tried to make their way back into my ear gates no longer had power over me. I had gotten my power back! This was what strangers were seeing. These people began voicing that I was inspiring and wanted to be part of the upcoming business venture I was working on. They were all about supporting in any way possible and still are. I had finally defeated my self-limitations. I had reintroduced myself to myself and to the world. In this, I found my purpose. I overcame so that others that are in their lowest of low places can overcome too. I was able to take the most hurtful insult spewed at me throughout my childhood and turn it into a business that makes women feel good about themselves and the brand they're wearing.

In this healing process, I've learned that God made us priceless and limitless. We have unlimited abilities from birth. And as we grow up, limits are placed on us through our family, society, and ourselves. With God, we can take the limits off. You can achieve anything your heart desires! Truly! But it all begins with getting yourself off the floor from that low place, true inner reflection and healing yourself one step at a time.

Ashley Johnson

Author bio

Ashley Johnson is a creative entrepreneur with an amazing vernacular for business, retail, and design. Having a keen eye for the qualities necessary in the support of a balanced portfolio, Ashley offers refinement, class, and reliability to a global market.

As the Owner and Creative Designer of Snob Flair Boutique, a conglomerate specializing in reintroducing women to themselves through fashion forward, feel-good pieces, Ashley inspires the importance of having unmatched productivity in an ever-changing business society.

Her goal is simple: the intentional boosting of femininity and confidence in the world of women by any means necessary.

Having a diversified gallery of entrepreneurial investments, Ashley is a consultant, reality expert, interior designer, and women's advocate.

When she is not out painting the town pink, she is an amazing wife, communal leader, and cherished mother of four.

Ashley Johnson. Creator. Mogul. Design Enthusiast.

I Am Not An Imposter!

~ Angel Riley

"Am I worthy of success?" I silently asked myself this question far too many times. Not because of a lack of confidence, but because I struggled to own my truth. *I AM* confident. *I AM* capable. *I AM* accomplished. So why am I second-guessing my career, financial, and sometimes relationship success?

I felt like a fraud. *At any moment, my façade would be exposed. I will be a laughingstock, never able to publicly show my face again.* My life successes are because of the grace of God. However, I often felt I was not qualified to be in the positions He placed me. Instead of giving thanks and asking God to order my steps, I tried to hide in the shadows. I barely took credit for my work, even if my feelings were hurt when others took credit without my permission. I attempted to surround myself with mediocre people, even if their self-imposed drama mentally exhausted me. I embraced my introvert characteristics, even if it meant opting out of an active social life. I did my best to become the world's first invisible person. I figured if no one realized I existed, I never needed to explain how I achieved various levels of success. I would never be exposed.

Unfortunately, my master "invisible woman" plan was seriously flawed. You see, I never recognized that *I AM* ambitious. Ambition can be compared to the little black dress: it fits perfectly; it unknowingly exudes confidence; it effortlessly commands attention; and it is dependable and the go-to for all occasions. The more I attempted to be invisible, the more my ambition showed up screaming "HERE I AM, put the spotlight on me!" I had no choice but to accept the moment and pray no one would find out I was a fake.

After spending a decade of feeling inadequate in my accomplishments, I learned the term *imposter syndrome.* According to Merriam Webster, *imposter syndrome* (originally called *imposter phenomenon*) is a false and sometimes crippling belief that one's success is the product of luck or fraud rather than skill.

I believe in God and attribute my successes to Him. For some reason, I did not believe God placed me in positions that aligned with my qualifications and skillset. Saying it out loud, I sound utterly ridiculous. But this is what I believed - God blessed an "imposter" with success.

Now that my condition has been revealed, how do I overcome the limiting belief? With much trial and error, I "control" imposter syndrome using eight techniques:

Call it out: Whenever I start doubting my success worthiness, I yell or write "imposter syndrome." This technique allows me to recognize my feelings are unwarranted. Here's a secret: I noticed imposter syndrome appears the strongest whenever I am unconsciously suppressing fear. I am not a fraud. I just may be afraid in the moment.

Go ahead and brag: Success is not happenstance. It is only achieved when you put in the work. I track my success in a *brag journal*. Each time a goal is accomplished, I write a summary or short story of the actions taken. Whenever I need a reminder that I am not a fake, I read a passage from my journal. The ability to reminisce on some of your proudest moments boosts your mood, increases your energy, and inspires you to keep moving forward.

Assemble the tribe: I believe I am only as strong as those around me. About 15 years ago, I attended a professional development conference where the keynote speaker stated everyone needs a personal board of directors. I rely on my tribe for support.

Ditch perfectionism: Striving for perfection sounds the imposter syndrome panic alarm. If I find myself sounding the alarm, I reflect on Sheryl Sandberg's quote: "Done is better than perfect." I am successful because I did it, not because I perfected it.

Say "no" to comparison: Comparison is the undefeated heavyweight champion. I refrain from believing my success is less than another person's success. I will never win the fight. If someone is on a similar success path as mine, I seek them out for mentorship.

Coaching is key: A life coach is the ultimate accountability partner. A coach can challenge you to be the best version of yourself; and help you build confidence. Working with a life coach is one of the many reasons I entered the coaching industry.

The power of *I AM*: Positive affirmations is the imposter syndrome kryptonite. Whenever I start proclaiming my positive attributes using the words *I AM,* my confidence becomes rock solid. I am literally conquering a limiting belief using the power of my words.

Check your faith: Once I made my spiritual life a priority, my struggle with imposter syndrome decreased significantly.

Am I worthy of success? YES! *I AM* not an imposter.

Angel Riley

Author Bio

Angel Riley always had a tremendous sensory for organizational leadership. When that talent was met with her radiant and empathic nature, she became a natural candidate for a career in life coaching and development. Having already attained a mastery of education in the realms of International Studies and Government Management, Angel was poised for helping the world at large to map out their everyday lives.

The Knowing

~ **Kamikazi Sabune-Sheriff**

When you grow up in a culture like mine; as an African born female child in Uganda, where children are only seen and not heard, you tend to quickly find the courage to be heard. I grew up afraid of everything. I was not encouraged to explore my environment, and neither was I engaged in conversations about making choices. Choices were made for me; from what to eat, when to sleep, what to wear, where to play, what items to play with, including whom to play with, My family's belief was about Love and Prayer being at the center of my upbringing. My grandfather was a clergyman and he made sure that the whole family was summoned in the living room for prayer and praise every evening after dinner. We attended church every Sunday; at least he and I did religiously. I believe that it was during that ritual that developed my yearning for spirituality. Regardless of my family's ritual to engage in prayer, I was nowhere near in the understanding of who God was or what I was really doing!

That is where the knowing in me began to emerge that God and church had something to do with one another. It occurred to me that the whole concept of going to church and prayers at home had more meaning than I could articulate at that young age of 4-5 years old. I cannot explain what those feelings were, but what I know now is that I developed an extraordinarily strong awareness of God's presence in my life, a spirit of love.

As a child, I know now that I wanted to embody my grandfather's image. I was drawn to his energy and that energy of spirituality was strongly infused. My grandfather was the representation of a father. I called him "papa." Who my biological father was, did not come into play at that time (still searching). I NEVER asked. But my grandfather substituted for the absence of a father. I was very content and very connected to him; we had a beautiful bond. He was my papa who adored me and I was enamored by him! The rest of the family was also on board with the same tenderness that my grandfather showed me; through hugs, kisses and the gentle care I was given by everyone who was in proximity. And my mother's own adoration for me was endearing to most and at the same time almost nauseating to others. As a young child from the ages of 2-6, I lived in a very trusting and most definitely a loving bubble. I trusted, I loved, and I believed in everyone and everything. I did not need courage, I had love, I had trust and how would courage play in this equation?

At 7 or 8 years old, I would wake up in a nightmare! My bubble shattered and my world, as I knew it, would never be the same, when I was sent to go live with an uncle, a single and wealthy father to my toddler cousin. Around the same time, my mother had also moved out of her parent's home where we all lived, and was now living in a serious relationship with a medical Dr., a man who had courted her from her father's home and made her his wife with whom she had two children. I later came to find out that my mother was also living in her own nightmare with this man, experiencing domestic violence in her home. My mother had decided to leave me with her parents.

It was during this time that COURAGE entered my life and became the formula I would always use in my incredibly young life. I believe courage is GOD! With COURAGE, I learned that I needed to call on BELIEF. With belief, I needed to find LOVE. I asked myself where and how would I find love, and I discovered that I needed to go to PRAYER. With prayer, I learned that I needed to visit FORGIVENESS. When I visited forgiveness, I found PEACE, JOY, and HAPPINESS. Today, when I experience any trials and tribulations, I quickly draw from that formula.

It is that formula of courage, belief, love, prayer, forgiveness, peace, joy, and happiness that continues to anchor me. It is that same formula that I spoke into existence when my beloved mother and my 2 brothers (ages 2 and 3) died. I was 13 years old. I felt pain that I could not explain. I was lost without my mother. Family members went on with their lives hoping I would snap out of "this," but the only solace I could find was to turn to God. I said out loud, "God, there's got to be a better place than this."

With my mother gone, I stopped talking (almost mute) and the only intervention was to bring my cousin who was the same age as me from another country to begin healing and engaging me in conversation. My cousin and I would only look at one another and know what the other one meant or wanted.

I never attended my mother's funeral. My mother, my 2 younger brothers (ages 2 and 3) and I were in a hit-and-run car accident while taking a walk. I have wondered to this day the reason l had been the only survivor. I attributed my survival to my formula. Having the audacity to BELIEVE that I have a purpose in this world. Having the audacity to LOVE. Having the audacity to PRAY. Having the audacity to have PEACE, JOY, and HAPPINESS, all gave me the COURAGE to keep on going, putting one foot in front of the other, taking moments at a time to remember my PURPOSE. My purpose is to sprinkle what God has given me to others. I live by that purpose today.

God heard me. I came to the United States of America. I graduated from High School, earned a bachelor's degree in psychology and a minor in Early Elementary Education, and then earned a master's degree in Social Work. Finally, I got married, had a son, and today, I can say that I have led with Uncommon Courage living in *grace, gratitude,* and feeling *blessed* for who I am.

Kamikazi Sabune-Sheriff

Author Bio

Kamikazi Sabune-Sheriff is known as Kami by family and friends. She has a Master's degree(MSW) from Silberman School of Social Work at Hunter College in New York, New York. Kami earned her BA degree in Psychology and a Minor in Early Elementary Education from New Jersey City University in Jersey City, NJ. She started a Life Coaching project to empower underprivileged women. She recently participated in a project called Seen and Heard by a well-known Cleveland Ohio photographer, Honey Lazar; that was on exhibit at Bowling Green State University in Cleveland Ohio, portraying Conversations on Sexual Assault, Abuse and Rape. Currently, Kami works for Cones Wesley Long Hospital supporting families with medical needs in Greensboro, NC. She is inspired by service, love, forgiveness, and kindness as her ritual for daily spiritual living. When Kami is not working, she tends to family, her body, mind, and spirit. Kami has a certificate in Reiki. She prides herself on being a great cook, organizer, and creative guru. She is a mother of a 20-year-old son whom she adores. She has a strong team of supportive women friends that cheer her on in her endeavors. Kami maintains to be grateful, living a blessed life.

Perfect is Never Perfect

~ Lori Cox

I sat on the couch watching tv and saw all these perfect women. Perfect shape, not fat, perfect skin tone; they were just perfect. I always wondered why I couldn't be the perfect woman. I watched as they smiled, hugged, and talked to each other. They didn't have a care in the world. I wondered how they did it; how they kept sane and positive thoughts. I guess being perfect doesn't come with any cons. I just wanted to be perfect. I knew that I wasn't.

I turned off the tv getting up from the couch, then took a deep breath and walked over to the full-sized mirror. I stared at myself. The face of disgust appeared on my face. I looked horrible. I didn't look like those women. I was ugly... I was fat... I was too dark. I hated it. No one liked this kind of appearance.

"God, I look horrible," I whispered to myself, then pulled up my shirt revealing my stomach. I had a horrible body. I had flab and lots of it. I didn't look anywhere near perfect.

I let go of my shirt letting it cover my stomach to avoid seeing it anymore. My body was something I was always self-conscious about and seeing all these beautiful women with perfect bodies never helped either. "You look horrible," I said to myself as I just stared in the mirror. "Two divorces and you're fat; you really think someone's gonna love you again?" I whispered to myself. "This is your fault," I said.

I was now in a state of mind where I always thought negatively. I never thought positively. I always doubted myself and never even believed in myself. I always tore myself down thinking about being divorced twice. All these things just added up and made me look horrible. These things made me look like a person no one wants, no one will love, or even talk to. My mind was in a very dark place no matter what time it was or what positive things people told me about myself. So much had happened to me in the last couple of years; thinking positive was not an option.

Then seeing all these women smiling with skinny bodies and beautiful skin tone made everything worse. I knew my future was not gonna be bright. I knew it was gonna be very dark, no matter what. I was prepared for that; I was prepared for the worst thoughts and for my body to get uglier over time.

I looked at myself once more in the mirror and became grossed out by what I saw. I turned around and walked back over to the couch. The self-doubt was kicking in more than ever. I wish I thought positively about myself. I was tired of hating myself. Everything I did I had something negative to say about it. "Lori, what's wrong with you?" I groaned staring at the blank tv. "Why do we have to do this to ourselves?" I whispered. "Why can't we just silence the past? We hate ourselves too much," I said. "Why can't we just feel good about ourselves?" I said. Talking to myself seemed like the only thing that would silent my mind for a couple of minutes. "I don't get why I can't love myself," I groaned then I remembered buying a skirt a couple of weeks ago. I never put it on because, well, I realized it would only look good on skinny people and not me. I got up from the couch once again, walked towards the stairs, and heading up to my room.

I looked around until I found the skirt. I got undressed and put it on, but cringed while doing that knowing I was going to look horrible. I zipped itt then walked over to the mirror. I wasn't ready, although I knew the outcome. I looked up at the mirror seeing myself and just stared at myself not knowing what to think or say. "Just try to think positive," I whispered to myself. I smoothed out the skirt, then doing a slight spin, "Ok, ok," I smiled.

"Will people think I look good?" I asked myself. I shook my head getting those thoughts out of my mind. As I looked in the mirror, I started thinking of the positive things. I realized my curves were looking pretty good in this skirt. "Ok, I look good." I laughed. "Where's the blouse?" I asked as I looked around my room till I found it. I pulled off my shirt and put the blouse on and I went back to the mirror. "Damn," I said to myself doing another spin. I did realize I should stop spinning before I got dizzy. "Why do I hate myself so much?" I whispered. "Damn, I do look good though." I smiled.

I looked at my skin and for once I looked like I was glowing in some type of way. The biggest thing was my skin color; I always thought I was too dark. Being in this outfit made me feel confident about myself somehow. "Your skin is beautiful," I told myself. "You're not fat; you have the curves. Two divorces, so what? You got this. Stop doubting yourself. We work hard and one day we will get what we have been working so hard for," I explained to myself.

This past year was the worst. I forgot that my opinion mattered, not a stranger's opinion. I forgot that my skin color was actually beautiful and it had its own beautiful glow. I had beautiful curves that women craved. I looked beautiful even though my past was nowhere near beautiful. The world put out a bold message that it only wanted a certain woman and she had to be skinny, with no flaws. While the rest of the women were put down - including me.

I began to start thinking positively again. I remind myself that one day someone will love me. One day women of every kind will get the proper love they deserve.

*I also have to remember that **perfect** is never **perfect**.*

Lori Ann Cox

Author Bio

Lori Ann has been writing since childhood, but she only became a published author in 2017. Spurred on by the therapeutic nature of written words, she has two bestselling anthologies under her name and has thus carved out a place for herself amidst veterans of personal development and self-help literature. She is also a serial entrepreneur and loves embarking on lucrative ventures just as much as she loves traveling to new places. She hails from Eastern North Carolina, and when she's neither writing, traveling, nor being a serial entrepreneur, you can find her reclining for a glass of wine with her wonderful husband.

Boundless Hope

~ **Lanashane Robert**

*"Out of suffering have emerged the strongest souls;
the most massive characters are seared with scars."*
—*Khalil Gibran*

When the Japanese mend broken objects, they aggrandize them by filling their cracks with gold. It is their belief that when something suffers damage it becomes beautiful—their understanding holds the truth that it's more valuable once broken. Restoring a broken object by enhancing its scars with real gold powder is referred to as *kintsugi*. The art proclaims that broken parts will never be diminished or disguised; a scar remains, but rather as an embellished design that exists to adorn the object with new beauty. A thought-provoking notion that can be applied to our lives ...

In a time of unfathomable global awakening, we appreciate that we, too, are *kintsugi* artworks. Although we tend to hide our flaws, wounds and broken parts, it's only through injury that healing ensues. We courageously accept and embrace the decision to not hide in the shadows of shame as we steadily embark on our journey, stronger than before. Scars, whether visible or invisible, are proof that we have overcome our difficulties—a beautiful metaphor for self-healing from the remnants of travesties. Our trials are laced with wisdom; they direct us to respect the inherent value within people and appreciate the potential they carry.

Once we value life without judgment, peace begins to cradle healing—gradually, we heal both our inner self and our outer world.

Kintsugi isn't only about mending broken objects with gold; instead, it embodies profound meaning and teachings surrounding our attitude towards life. It speaks to charming resilience and sublime confidence against an appreciation of beauty in imperfection. As we stand on the brink of change, this ancient belief holds true whilst we start to piece our lives and dreams together. The jagged lines are scars proudly flaunted to reflect the light. Unequivocally ... amidst traces of brokenness ... hope, faith and courage are tenanted—inherently turning our pain into power!

Lonely in our minds, we argue the cruelty of our plight, too afraid to share our dreaded thoughts with the world. Oblivious that the transformational gateway of higher awareness shapes our tenacity in preparation for endings and encourages the blossoming of new beginnings—ushered in with grace to fulfill our destiny. Helmed with inner knowing, we set our potential and confidence in alignment with our goals to give our dreams wings.

We are not perfect beings; we are known to attempt things—make mistakes and often stumble and fall. But we are also a species known to rise after a fall and persist to learn and grow. *Kintsugi* is a powerful metaphor that encourages us to showcase our scars proudly and celebrate the person we have become through joy and sadness—a paradox of emotions to be lauded for the lessons that inspirit growth. Strong people break, yet they don't stay broken. They have a remarkable tenacity to piece themselves back together whilst mending their wounds, all the while knowing that courage is never born without fear. Fear undoubtedly is the quintessential component upon which courage is cultivated. While mistakes serve to pilot us to a better place, and once we enkindle our potential, define and restore action everything changes. By learning to swing our sword of truth, owning it without hesitation, helps free us from all that has held us back.

Like any warrior, we come back stronger.

Own your steely determination to set sail on a new route, pledge to own your story and unbridle yourself from its previous mastery over you.

Wisdom is appreciating the contradiction that the greatest growth occurs at the border of pleasure and pain or order and chaos. Let neither pain nor pleasure interfere with your pursuit of your purpose. Only when you embrace the potential of believing in yourself will you defeat all the enemies that held you prisoner. In one fell swoop, you erase self-inflicted mental barriers that debilitated your growth.

Strong women stare down fear, graced with hope and resilience, despite the storms around them. They always learning to reframe their thoughts and be focused, to be armored with courage and led by intention.

Let the wounds and pain you so carefully hide from the world play out so that you can transform. The scars you have, whether visible or not, are your trophies of survival that speak of the fierce fight you fought to be here. Bruises and scars eventually fade, but your battles won't be for naught. You are hemmed with a knowing and confidence, chaperoned by a vision fashioned out of faith, that enables you to advocate your worth. Rise and be propelled by the energy from the depths of your soul. The relationship you develop with yourself has an incredible ability to set the tone for every other relationship you may initiate. Remain unapologetically committed to your goals and letting go of the opinions and judgements of others—stand tall and let the giant within you take its place.

You have everything you need within you for the success that lies in wait for you.
As seen in nature, a tiny seed holds within its casing the potential of a huge tree. For the seed to deliver on

its greatest expression, it must be cracked open; it sacrifices itself to give way to something new. This phenomenon is best understood by those who accept the process of growth.

What hurts you today holds the empowering gift of making you stronger tomorrow. Before you know it, you will be ready to step into your wish fulfillment with a new zest to ascend.

You are not just a woman ... you are a WARRIOR!!!

Unflinchingly assent to your heart and soul leading the way; they know best, of your renowned character that was written in the narrative of your life.

Unimpeachably, it is time for the re-emergence of your authentic self—as a fierce, formidable, forceful and phenomenal woman—an exquisite masterpiece contoured by boundless hope!

Lanashane Robert

Author Bio

After years as a communication specialist and senior manager in telecoms, Lanashane ventured into establishing self-owned businesses. Her flourishing potential has awarded her the title of designer and artist of her jewellery brand. Lanashane's creations have featured at international art exhibitions, and she has been invited to participate in international fashion weeks. Her determination and passion to inspire and motivate people has paved the way for her novel. A woman of resilient courage and high accomplishments, Lanashane is beautifully steered by her soul purpose.

Women of
Courage Honoree

Min. Nakita Davis

What does a Woman of Courage mean to YOU?
"A Woman of courage is *BOLD* even when others tell her to back down. She helps her fellow Queens in the midst of adversity.

She's positioned, poised, and equipped to do the job.
A Woman of Courage looks FEAR in the face and laughs~ even if she's scared; because she *KNOWS* that *God is with her!*"

BIO
Min. Nakita Davis is the Proud CEO & Founder of Jesus, Coffee, and Prayer Christian Publishing House LLC; an International Best-Selling Publisher, Author, sought-after Motivational Speaker, Marketing/Media & PR maven. She helps Women of Faith to Drop the Excuses and Play their Royal Position in the home and the marketplace by helping them produce their Best-Selling books; Step on Global Stages, and increase their visibility, credibility, and authority in the marketplace. She is married to her childhood sweetheart and has 2 beautiful children. They reside in Atlanta, GA.

Social Media

FB - https://www.facebook.com/jesuscoffeeandprayer

IG -https://www.instagram.com/jesuscoffeeandprayer

Schedule Your Best-Selling Book/Marketing Consultation Now

https://calendly.com/jesuscoffeeandprayer/best-selling-book-consultation

Website: https://www.jesuscoffeeandprayer.com

Join our Speaker Author Girl Boss Private FB Group

FB - https://www.facebook.com/groups/speakerauthorgirlbosses

Ashley Hudson

What does a Woman of Courage mean to YOU?
A woman of courage is someone who unapologetically walks in her purpose. She is a woman who defies the odds against her and expresses her authentic self. She gracefully and humbly embraces change around her.

BIO
Ashley Hudson is a blogger, speaker, and award-winning dentist with a passion for seeing women walk in authenticity and God given purpose! She does this through her writing at Undoubted Grace, an online community of working moms learning to enjoy and embrace their individual stories of motherhood.
She coaches overwhelmed women in balancing work and family life, practicing intentional self-care and cultivating spiritual growth. Using the firm foundation instilled in her from childhood as a guide, Ashley spends most of her time learning in her most rewarding mission, creating a nurturing Christ-centered home for her family.

Social Media

Website - www.undoubtedgrace.com

FB - www.facebook.com/undoubtedgrace

IG - www.instagram.com/undoubtedgrace

Aimee Clute

What does a Woman of Courage mean to YOU?
I want people to know that even in the face offer, lack, inadequacy, any type of adversity; that they can do anything. If they will mix their faith with God's word they will be UNSTOPPABLE! There is nothing more gratifying than knowing that you are walking out God's purpose for your life!

BIO
Dr. Clute is an ordained minister holding a Doctorate in Divinity and Certificate of Chaplaincy with 40 years of ministerial experience. She is an award-winning Gospel recording artist having sung all over the world and on major television networks. Other rolls in her life include being an author, co-pastor, wife, mother, and grandmother.

Social Media
Website - www.aimeeclute.net
FB - Dr. Aimee Clute FB - Aimee Clute Ministries
IG- Aimee Clute

Dr. Shelia Rivers

What does a Woman of Courage mean to YOU?
Sharing with other women the courage to have the courage.

BIO
I'm Dr. Shelia Rivers, DSW, LCSW, MPH trauma expert for Women. I have been a mental health professional for 13 years. I wear numerous professional hats, such as being the CEO and Chief Therapist of Rivers Psychotherapy Services, published author, Adjunct Professor at Tulane University, Public Speaker, Expert Mental Health Consultant, Social Work Intern Supervisor, and Licensed Clinical Social Worker.

Social Media
Website - www.RiversPsychotherapyServices.com
www.SheliaRivers.com
FB - www.facebook.com/Dr-Shelia-Rivers-418425445394215 |
www.facebook.com/Rivers-Psychotherapy-Services-PLLC-1655779518031290

LinkedIn - www.linkedin.com/in/dr-shelia-rivers-dsw-lcsw-mph-53b5ba19/

Hanna Marmalich

What does a Woman of Courage mean to YOU?

I'm scared yet I'm willing to do it" is the tag line attached to my life. I have had to learn to ignore fear's dialog and go for the goal that fear says I am unworthy of. Whether it be a new opportunity, a new friendship, or simply going backwards to start something over again, I can shun fear and courageously go forward and do the thing that looks hard, impossible, and out of reach.

BIO

Hanna Marmalich is an International Best-Selling Author, mental health advocate, writer, and overseer at Safe Harbor Clinic; a thriving Outpatient Mental Health and Addiction Center in Long Beach, Mississippi. One of her favorite ways to exude servant leadership, is through the unyielding influence of social media. Hanna is the curator of Seasons of Grace by Hanna Lorraine, a faith-based Instagram page created in congruence with her self-published devotional, to encourage believers in the "thick of life"; to get through difficult times by the power of a flourishing relationship with God. Her inspirational content has touched many, as thousands of online followers engage weekly, in the anticipation of the selfless exhortation provided through Hanna's content.

Social Media

IG - @hanna_lorraine

Shadaria Allison

What does a Woman of Courage mean to YOU?
Women of Courage lead with the truth. Understanding that everything that happens to you; happens for you and is shaping your inner strength as you live.

BIO
Shadaria Allison is a 2-time best-selling author, speaker, and women's enthusiast. Her portfolio reflects a millennial entrepreneur of epic proportions; stewarding a myriad of professional and creative vernaculars; ranging from beauty, modeling, and PR-consulting; to social media management, freelance writing services, and content design. Affectionately known as:

"Dr. Allison The Beauty Practitioner"™, Shadaria Allison merges seamless creativity, with a heart for people; a trait she refuses to compromise throughout her career.

Social Media
Website - www.drallison911.com/
FB - https:/ www.facebook.com/doc.allison.73
IG - @drallison911
LinkedIn - www.linkedin.com/in/shadaria-allison-80696b112/

Pastor Berlinda A. Hart Love

What does a Woman of Courage mean to YOU?
A woman of courage is someone with the tenacity and will to overcome obstacles knowing that she will survive and be victorious. She knows how to trust in God to bring her through the most challenging times in her life and nothing can prevent her from achieving her dreams. Her attitude determines her altitude, she is always positive, and she believes in being a blessing to others. Her energy and spirit are an inspiration to others.

BIO
I retired from the Trenton Public School District in New Jersey after 31 years as administrator and teacher. Additionally, I am a graduate of three institutions of higher learning: Princeton Theological Seminary (MDiv); Rider University (MA); and The College of New Jersey (BS), and have authored three books: Coping with my Mother's Stroke, A Daughter's Story; My Mother's Stroke and Miracle Recovery; and Sermons from the Heart, A Collection of Divinely

Inspired Devotional Sermons, A Special Tribute. Several of my articles have been published by my local newspaper, the Valdosta Daily Times. Also, I have served the African Methodist Church for 22 years, and have pastored 3 congregations, my current charge being Payton AME Church in Valdosta, GA.The epitome of my career has been my role as a caregiver for my parents until their demise.

Social Media
Twitter - @Loveberlinda1A
FB – www.facebook.com/anietalove
LinkedIn - www.linkedin.com/in/rev-dr-berlinda-a-hart-love-b6386633
Church - paytonamechurch@gmail.com

Lanetta & Mela Singleton

What does a Woman of Courage mean to YOU?
A Woman of Courage is one who perseveres against all odds. Although life may come at her fast and hard, she is able to take control and make it look easy while doing it.

BIO
Founded by two sisters, Ethereal Flow, LLC was birthed in Greenville, SC and started as a mere concept in the atmosphere. As we browsed through stores and online sites looking for swimwear that was edgy, yet sophisticated and classy, we fell short on these findings. Products were either too expensive for the average consumer or too cheap and of bad quality. There was no real in-between. Our store bridges that gap – expensive looks at affordable prices.

Social Media
Website - www.efswim.com
FB - www.facebook.com/etherealflowswim/
IG - www.instagram.com/
etherealflowswim?igshid=1nocaukc0785d

Lisa Parsons

What does a Woman of Courage mean to YOU?
At the heart of courage is a willingness to face one's authentic self. When we acknowledge both our strengths and our weaknesses we come to the crossroads of change. Courage not only takes the first step but continues step by step for as long as it takes to make it a lasting change.

BIO
I have over 10 years experience in helping individuals who are struggling through trauma and anxiety to regain confidence and discover the true life they have been created for. I currently meet with clients through telehealth and in office at Safe Harbor Clinic in Long Beach, MS.

Social Media
Website – www.Insightswithlisa.co
LinkedIn - Lisa Nelson

Brittany Thompson

What does a Woman of Courage mean to YOU?
Woman of Courage means taking a step beyond our comfortable zone. It means to be in constant never-ending pursuit of purpose. Its the elimination of excuses and living with the standard of status quo. Once we identify ourselves and accept the call of leadership, we inevitable give up the right to be average and ordinary.

BIO
I am a wife of 12 years to my middle school sweetheart, Leon. Together we have 3 children ages 10, 9, and 3. We consider ourselves co-preneurs who invest in residential and commercial real estate as well as educate others to do the same. Lastly, we live a vision based life that is outlined by God and heavily influenced by His purpose and our passion.

Social Media
Website - www.lbthompsongroup.com
FB - www.facebook.com/lbthompsongroup14
IG - www.instagram.com/therealbjt/
LinkedIn - www.linkedin.com/in/brittany-thompson/

Latrina McCarty

What does a Woman of Courage mean to YOU?
Being a Woman of Courage means the ability to be resilient. "Take it all one day at a time and enjoy the journey" by Kristi Barlett. This is what I have chosen to live by. Life may seem unfair sometimes. One may even question... "Why me? Resiliency is the ability to pause for a moment and then "keep it going." A Woman of Courage means you realize the ability that is already within you and the courage to embrace its strength to move forward. In "Olivia's Journey," Olivia discovered that the very thing she was searching for was already inside of her.

BIO
Latrina R. Graves McCarty is an author, playwright, and is currently a high school English teacher. Ms. McCarty has taught creative writing, drama, journalism as well as speech and debate. She earned a bachelor's degree in broadcast journalism and speech communication, holds a Master of Education in English, and is currently seeking a Doctorate of

Philosophy in Mass Communication. Latrina found her passion/her purpose/her why when she lost her best friend, her husband in 2010. She is empowering women by sharing her new journey through her fictional novel, "Olivia's Journey."

Social Media
Website - www.latrinamccarty.org
FB: Author and Playwright Latrina Graves McCarty, Mississippi Speaker Connection, and Off The Court by LGM Productions, LLC
IG - Author Trina G Mac
LinkedIn - Latrina R. Graves McCarty

Sabrina Stallworth

What does a Woman of Courage mean to YOU?
My perception of a woman of Courage is- one of determination, unafraid to step outside of the lines, willing to commit in helping others to move forward in their greatness!. A woman of courage is unapologetic in doing what's ethically correct!.

BIO
Sabrina Stallworth, a native of Biloxi, MS., grew up in Atlanta, GA. A self-taught artisan, who's median in her art work is bottles. Sabrina is also a designer of custom accessories: handbags, jewelry, belts sandals, and wallets. Sabrina is a executive board trustee at the Ohr-O'Keefe Museum of Art.
Sabrina also enjoys teaching leather working.

Social Media
Website - AllBottledUpByBre.Biz
Facebook- AllBottledUpByBre
Instagram- Allbottledup1

Thettra Brown-Shugart

What does a Woman of Courage mean to YOU?
What Women of Courage means to me, I believe
courage is the moral strength to look fear in the face
and say, "I will not yield to you."

BIO
Thettra Brown-Shugart, is a native of Charleston SC.
She has an education in esthetician, from the
Academy of Cosmetology Institute, and a Business
accounting education from Miller Motte Technical
College. While working for Ulta Cosmetics Thettra told
her coworker that she will have her own cosmetic line
one day, and that was the beginning of "Forever So
Beautiful." With her education, experienced
background, and training in Smash Box, Urban
Decay, Bare Essential, Iman and Color Me Beautiful
Cosmetics. Thettra also decided to pick up a desire
that has always been in her heart, which is now
photography. Thettra has now become known as a
celebrity photography in her city of Charleston, SC.
Despite being known as a celebrity photographer she
understands that Photographer is her ministry.

Taking photos and seeing how my clients faces light up let's me understands it's not about me it's about the story I'm creating and memories. For my women I'm able to do makeup and Photography.

Forever So Beautiful goals are to launch products and services globally and 6to open cross the world. When you think of beauty and photography, think of "Forever So Beautiful" because we are all "Forever So Beautiful."

Social Media
Website - www.foreversobeautiful.com
Facebook - Forever So Beautiful

Tonya Williams

What does a Woman of Courage mean to YOU?
A woman of courage is a woman who is passionate about walking in her purpose even if she has to do it scared & alone. She's not afraid to take chances and invest in herself because there's always a return!

BIO
Certified Life Coach in the areas of Spiritual, Financial & Relational. Podcast Host of Fierce, Favored & Spiritually Grounded, Public Speaker, Mentor, Influencer, Author of The Best Version of Me.

Social Media
Website - https:/ mymentor.life/
FB - Spiritually_Grounded
IG - Tonya Williams Life Coach
LinkedIn - Tonya Williams

INEZ HALL-WILLIAMS

What does a Woman of Courage mean to YOU?
It is a way for women to unite and encourage each other. We are to support and uplift one another.

BIO
I am a wife of twenty-three years, we have two sons ages nineteen and fifteen. I am a minister, teacher, coach, friend. I am a person of my word.

Social Media
Website - www.mythirtyone.com/206066

Liz Hoop

What does a Woman of Courage mean to YOU?

It has been said that wisdom grows from places of great adversity. Engineered to help others find their way out; is philanthropic liaison, Liz Hoop.

Liz Hoop is an International Best-Selling Author, speaker, communal leader, and tenured liaison with Solace Hospice. Professionalism, being the minimum standard in all she does, Liz attributes the cause of people; her greatest trademark. Having served many years at an executive level, in the areas of Marketing and Management; it has been a common thread of people-centric ethics that has ushered Liz into the vastness of philanthropy, overall.

Liz' motto is simple: Selflessly give your time and best efforts for the betterment of others; on purpose

BIO

Life is always unpredictable, and it can get downright scary sometimes. Daily stresses and challenges can certainly wear us down and then when something big happens—a job loss, an illness, a painful breakup—suddenly, things look a lot different in our lives and challenges can certainly wear us down and then when something big happens—a job loss, an illness, a painful breakup—suddenly, things look a lot different in our lives. Someone with courage is bold and brave, unafraid to face tough challenges.

Having courage means acting when others are afraid of the danger, or simply acting without fear of failure.

Social Media

Website - www.solacehospice.net/

FB - www.facebook.com/lizhoop

IG – www.instagram.com/lthoop

LinkedIn – www.linkedin.com/in/lhoop

Frances Jones

What does a Woman of Courage mean to YOU?

A woman of courage means stepping out in faith despite what may be occurring in your life. Courage is birthed through adversity but the desire to move forward is arise through the determination to use your life experiences to help someone else.

BIO

Frances Jones holds master's degrees from the University of Mississippi in accounting and educational leadership. She is a Certified professional coach, Energy Leadership Index master practitioner, and the founder of Heart Desires Fulfillment Coaching, LLC. She specializes in infertility coaching and has more than twenty years of personal infertility experience. She uses her story and the empowering lessons she learned to inspire, motivate, encourage, and help others who are dealing with negative emotions and stigmas associated with fertility challenges. Frances lives in Memphis, Tennessee, with her family.

Social Media

Website - www.heartdesirescoaching.com
FB & IG - @heartdesirescoaching

Tina Ramsay

What does a Woman of Courage mean to YOU?
A Woman of Courage is a Leader, Trailblazer, and Motivator. She embodies determination within herself to be Fearless and Never Gives Up.

BIO
#1 Best Selling-International Author, Creator & Host of The Tina Ramsay TV Show & International Podcast. The Promoter of Brands, Connector, and Developer of Opportunities for Entrepreneurs to Shine, Share, and Grow!

Social Media
Website - TheTinaRamsayShow.com
FB - The Tina Ramsay Show
IG - The Tina Ramsay Show

Brandi Thompson

What does a Woman of Courage mean to YOU?
A woman of courage steps out in faith and tackles hard decisions. She goes against the grain and the world. She is bold about her convictions and in growing the kingdom of God.

BIO
Brandi is a daughter of the King, wife, and mother to 7! She uses her creative skills to spread the gospel using makeup, skincare, and fashion, through social media.
Brandi has helped more than 200 women feel as beautiful as God made them.

Social Media
FB - www.facebook.com/mrs.thompson528
FB- www.facebook.com/makeupandmission
IG - www.instagram.com/makeupandmission

Yvonne Brown

What does a Woman of Courage mean to YOU?

A woman of courage is not for the faint of heart. It takes a strong and bold determination to walk into the divine assignment God has specifically carved out for me. The call is greater than any emotional feeling that may arise. As a woman of courage I know who I am and WHOSE I AM - A Daughter Of the Most High!

Therefore, though my path towards greater may encounter some valleys, as a Woman of Courage I am already arm to take the limits o immediately. Why? Because I Believe In My Greatness.

BIO

Yvonne Brown, a native of Philadelphia, Pennsylvania is making her mark as a Women Empowerment Coach. She is driven by a desire to help women to soar beyond their past to become the best versions of themselves. As a project manager for over ten years, Yvonne frequently found herself being a source of support and knowledge for other women in the workplace and other areas of her life. In 2020, she decided to launch a coaching business to be able to fully utilize her gift and to be accessible to even more women.

Because positive affirmations played a major role in her personal journey, Yvonne shares messages of empowerment through a t- shirt line (Myndful Tees Boutique) of affirming words encouraging women to believe that they are loved, deserve happiness and are enough. She also o ers courses to support women in reaching their goals through the A rm & Pursue Academy, focusing on self-love, money matters and the pursuit of purpose. She is the co-author of two amazing anthology projects, Our Truth Is Not A Lie and The Evolution E ect and plans to author more books for her audience and create retreats of healing and restoration for women.

Social Media

Website - www.armandpursueacademy.com

FB - www.facebook.com/yvonnebrownexhales/

IG - https://www.instagram.com/ yvonnebrownexhales

Diahann James

What does a Woman of Courage mean to YOU?
A woman of courage to me means, she has accessed her strength within, and decided to step out of her norm to make a change in her life, knowing her outcome will be better. She realizes her love for herself and for others and decides she will not let anything or anyone stop her from reaching forward. A woman of courage is a woman who believes she deserves better and go gets it.

BIO
Diahann James, New York born, graduate of Pace University, author, educator, entrepreneur, mother of two young adults, and a Mimi. Owning a daycare for 17 years, her love for children encouraged her to write a children's book. When she is not writing you can find her crocheting, taking nature walks or playing with her grandson.

Tye Miles

What does a Woman of Courage mean to YOU?

A woman of courage is a woman who knows what she wants to experience in life. She is courageous enough to believe she can have what she desires regardless of circumstance and the opinions of others. She is unstoppable in her pursuit of reaching her highest potential.

BIO

Tye Miles is a Certified Personal Coach, Business Strategist, Personal Branding Expert, International Speaker & Entrepreneur. She is the creator of personal development brand, FierceHER Woman and founder of Womens Well-Being Firm. Tye's passion: To empower women and women entrepreneurs to create a meaningful life aligned with their personal values, passion, and purpose.

Social Media

Website - www.wwwb rm.com

FB - www.facebook.com/ thetyemiles/?tsid=0.6470713307228944&source=re sult

IG - www.instagram.com/thetyemiles/
Website - www.woodandroyalty.com
FB - www.facebook.com/pro
le.php?id=100660245072268&ref=content_lter
www.instagram.com/woodandroyalty/

Sonya Smith

What does a Woman of Courage mean to YOU?

We have all heard the saying, "when life throws you lemons make lemonade". Such a profound statement to encourage a positive, I can do all things attitude during adversity and hardship. I must have made gallons of lemonade throughout my spiritual journey. Some sour, some bitter, and my best lemonade by far has been sweet and refreshing to the pallet of my life.

BIO

The true funnel toward effective leadership, is service. Embodying that preface with the highest of honor; is servant leader, Sonya Smith, an International Best-Selling Author, Speaker, Lieutenant, and Pastoral advocate for the Salvation Army in Mobile, Alabama. Pastor Smith submits that her faith in God and love; is her primary inspiration for being a change agent in this world.

Social Media

Stay Connected with Sonya Smith

FB - https://www.facebook.comprofile.php?id=100017891340908

Ashley Robertson

What does a Woman of Courage mean to YOU?

A woman of courage to me means a woman who has been through hardship & was afraid to go through it, yet she had the courage to do it anyway. She is someone who may have hesitated before but her weaknesses had made her stronger to not let fear cause her to be idle in the success she seeks. She is someone who isn't afraid to be brave & do what needs to be done to be successful. A woman of courage is a woman of confidence, & she may feel scared on the inside, but she will not let that stop her from being courageous. She will stop at nothing to do what she knows needs to be done.

BIO:

In a generation most exposed to the chains of mental health disparities, there is a voice of advocacy, in the likes of Ashley Robertson. Ashley is a compassionate leader, speaker, author, and mental health advocate. To accompany a passion for mental health advocacy, Ashley is a professional photographer at her own company, J & A Robertson Photography LLC, a beauty enthusiast with Red Aspen, jewelry consultant with Kole Jax Designs, and a beloved, pageant title holder. Recently reigning, as Mrs. Gulf 2020, Ashley uses her platform in pageantry, to bring awareness to mental health struggles, and to stop; once and for all, the sigma placed on those diagnosed with mental illness.

Social Media:

www.facebook.com/redaspenbeautyqueen (Red Apsen)

www.redsapenlove.com/ashleyrobertson

www.facebook.com/robertsonphotos (Photography)

www.facebook.com/authorashleyrobertson (Author)